I0063299

Beyond the Bedside:

The Transition to Nurse Leader

Dylan Salrin, MSN, RN, ONC-A

Published by Fairchild Union Press

ISBN: 979-8-218-84293-2

© 2025 Dylan Salrin. All rights reserved.

CONTENTS

CONTENTS

Part III: Empowering Teams

Part IV: Leading in the Bigger Picture

ACKNOWLEDGMENTS

To my mentors and teammates over the years—your guidance, support, and collaboration have shaped the experiences that form the foundation of this book. Thank you for inspiring me to grow, lead, and share these lessons.

THE PATH THAT LED ME HERE

Leadership is not something I originally sought out, it's something that I grew into, shaped by experiences, mentors, and challenges along the way. When I began my nursing career, my focus was on mastering the technical skills, providing compassionate care, and supporting my peers. Leadership seemed like an abstract concept, a distant role reserved for those who were more seasoned or ambitious. I didn't see myself as a leader then, but the seeds were being planted even in those early days.

One of the most pivotal moments in my journey came when I was fortunate enough to work under a manager who saw potential in me that I had yet to discover. She was more than a supervisor; she was a mentor who guided me onto a trajectory I didn't even know I wanted at the time. Her belief in my abilities, even when I doubted myself, became a powerful force in my growth. She encouraged me to take on challenges that stretched my skills, asked questions that deepened my thinking, and gave me opportunities to lead, all while providing unwavering support. Looking back, I realize how instrumental her guidance was in shaping the leader I am today.

I realized leadership might be part of my path when I took part in research projects. This experience became a foundation I built upon, allowing me to mentor others through initiatives like the clinical ladder, chairing committees focused on shared governance and policy reform, and, most significantly, precepting. These opportunities showed me how leadership can be about empowering others while driving meaningful change.

As my career progressed, I transitioned from a staff

position within the peri-operative services department to a Clinical Education Specialist. In this role, I focused on developing incoming staff, measuring competencies and skills, and teaching AORN's Peri-Op 101. I found myself not only drafting schedules but also hosting seminars and in-services, all while navigating the unique challenges that come with supporting the growth and development of a diverse group. These experiences solidified my passion for leadership and reinforced the idea that, when guided by purpose, leadership is an extension of the care we provide as nurses.

Over time, that path expanded. Today, I serve as an ASC Administrator and Director of Nursing, where the scope of leadership extends beyond education and mentorship to include operational strategy, financial stewardship, compliance, and the overall effectiveness of an ambulatory surgery center. This role has challenged me to balance the clinical lens I developed as a bedside nurse with the administrative responsibilities of guiding a team, ensuring quality outcomes, and sustaining organizational growth. It is a role that demands both vision and pragmatism. Its is also one that reminds me daily why the foundations of leadership I learned early in my career remain essential.

I began to notice patterns in the way I approached challenges. I found joy in mentoring new nurses, refining workflows, and advocating for change that improved outcomes and team morale. These experiences taught me that leadership is less about authority and more about influence. It is about inspiring those around you to strive for excellence while offering support and guidance.

Stepping into a formal leadership role was both exciting and daunting. I wrestled with imposter syndrome, questioning whether I was truly qualified to guide others. But every mistake I made, every doubt I overcame, became part of my growth. I learned that leadership isn't about perfection; it's about authenticity, humility, and the courage to learn alongside your team.

This book is a reflection of the journey I've taken and the lessons I've learned. It's a guide for those who, like me, find themselves navigating the transition from bedside nurse to leader. My hope is that these pages will provide you with practical tools, meaningful insights, and the inspiration to embrace your own unique leadership journey. Leadership is a path (not a destination) and every step you take shapes the impact you'll have on those you lead and serve.

Part I: The Foundations of Leadership

1

THE LEADER WITHIN YOU

Why Leadership Starts Within

Leadership is not about having all the answers or holding the loudest voice in the room. It starts with a deep understanding of yourself, your strengths, weaknesses, values, and motivations. Before you can effectively lead others, you must first lead yourself. This chapter will guide you through the process of self-awareness, help you recognize the unique traits that make you a leader, and provide actionable tools to overcome challenges like imposter syndrome.

Understanding Self-Awareness in Leadership

Leadership begins with knowing who you are and how you show up in different environments. Self-awareness is the foundation of emotional intelligence and effective decision-making. It involves understanding:

- Your Strengths and Weaknesses: Knowing what you excel at and where you need support is key to building a complementary team.
- Your Triggers and Reactions: Recognizing situations that challenge you emotionally helps you respond thoughtfully instead of reacting impulsively.

5

- Your Core Values: These are your guiding principles. When decisions align with your values, you lead authentically.

Expanded Insight: Take a moment to identify three strengths you consistently bring to your team. Then, consider one area where you could grow. How have these influenced your interactions with others?

Recognizing Your Unique Leadership Traits

No two leaders are the same, and that uniqueness is a strength. Your leadership style is shaped by your experiences, personality, and how you approach challenges. Some leaders are visionaries, naturally inclined to inspire and guide others toward a shared goal. Others excel as executors, focusing on achieving measurable results and ensuring tasks are completed efficiently. Still, some thrive as supporters, lifting their team members and creating an environment where everyone feels valued. Recognizing your natural tendencies allows you to refine your leadership approach and leverage your strengths effectively.

As a nurse, you've already honed critical skills such as empathy, clear communication, and the ability to manage crises. These are qualities that naturally translate into strong leadership. These traits, developed through hands-on patient care and collaboration with multidisciplinary teams, form the foundation of your unique leadership style. Embracing these attributes helps you lead with authenticity and confidence, setting you apart as a trusted and effective leader.

Confronting Imposter Syndrome

Imposter syndrome is the internal belief that you're not good enough or that you don't deserve your success. It's common among new leaders, especially in nursing, where perfectionism often reigns. Here's how to combat it:

- Recognize the Signs: Feelings of self-doubt, over-preparation, or attributing success to luck are red flags.
- Reframe Your Thinking: Instead of seeing leadership as a role you must master immediately, view it as a skill you're continuously building.
- Celebrate Small Wins: Leadership is a journey. Acknowledge milestones along the way, even the small ones.

Stepping into a leadership role, particularly in a new setting or as an external hire, can lead to significant self-doubt. Leaders may question their ability to guide a team effectively, regardless of how much preparation they've undertaken. What often helps is reflecting on the qualities and achievements that earned them the role: dedication to patient care, experience in research and presentations, involvement in committees, or maybe the ability to connect with colleagues. By focusing on these strengths, leaders can overcome self-doubt and recognize that they often know more than they initially give themselves credit for.

It is also important to remember a message echoed by many seasoned leaders: "Don't ever let someone make you feel like you don't belong." As a new leader, it is natural to compare yourself to peers who may have more exposure or familiarity in the space. But exposure is not the same as worthiness. Your seat at the table was not given... it was earned. Rapid changes in responsibility can make you feel overwhelmed, but they are not evidence that you are undeserving. Belonging in leadership comes from authenticity, not perfection.

Actionable Tool: Write down a recent success in your career. Break it down into steps and actions you took to achieve it. This process can help you see the tangible evidence of your leadership abilities.

Building Confidence as a Nurse Leader

Confidence doesn't always mean to be without doubt; it means trusting yourself to navigate challenges despite uncertainty. Building confidence starts with setting realistic goals that focus on manageable tasks while contributing to larger objectives. This approach prevents feeling overwhelmed and allows you to celebrate incremental progress. Seeking feedback is another essential step, as constructive criticism from trusted colleagues helps you grow and affirms your strengths. Additionally, practicing self-compassion is key. Leadership is a learning process, and you won't always get everything right. When mistakes happen, treat yourself with the same kindness you would offer a friend, using the experience as an opportunity to learn.

Reflect on a time when you overcame a challenge as a nurse. What qualities helped you succeed, and how can you apply those strengths to your leadership role? To lead others effectively, you must invest in your own growth.

Journaling is a powerful strategy for self-reflection, allowing you to document your leadership experiences, challenges, and insights on a daily or weekly basis.

Strengths-based development is another effective approach. Tools like Gallup's Clifton Strengths help you identify and build on your natural talents, giving you a clearer understanding of what sets you apart as a leader. Mentorship also plays a vital role in leadership development. A good mentor provides guidance, challenges your thinking, and offers the support needed to navigate your leadership journey with confidence.

Case Study: Emma, a new nurse manager, struggled with delegating tasks because she felt responsible for everything. Through journaling, she identified this tendency as a lack of trust in her team's capabilities. Her mentor helped her develop a plan to delegate incrementally, building her team's confidence and her own.

Leadership is a journey of continuous self-discovery. By understanding your unique traits, confronting self-doubt, and investing in personal growth, you lay the foundation for authentic, impactful leadership.

Reflection Prompts:

What personal values guide your leadership decisions?

_____

_____

_____

_____

_____

_____

How has imposter syndrome shown up in your career, and how have you addressed it?

_____

_____

_____

_____

_____

_____

What steps will you take to grow as a leader in the next 30 days?

_____

_____

_____

_____

_____

_____

Actionable Steps:

1. Schedule time this week for self-reflection or journaling.

2. Identify one area for growth and find a resource (book, mentor, course) to address it.

3. Celebrate one leadership success, no matter how small, to reinforce your confidence.

Notes:

_____

_____

_____

_____

_____

_____

_____

_____

_____

_____

_____

_____

_____

_____

_____

2

CARING IS ONLY HALF THE BATTLE

Leadership Beyond Caring

Nurses are often defined by their compassion. After all, it is a critical quality in patient care. However, leadership in nursing requires more than empathy. It demands clinical expertise, strategic thinking, and the ability to make evidence-based decisions. As a nurse leader, you must master the art of balancing care with competence to inspire trust, create effective teams, and achieve sustainable results. In this chapter, we'll explore how to bridge this gap and develop a leadership style that is both empathetic and effective.

Balancing Compassion with Competence

Compassion is the foundation of nursing, but competence is what drives results. Leaders who balance these two qualities can address both the emotional and operational needs of their teams. For example, when team conflicts arise, a compassionate leader listens to all sides and validates feelings, but an effective leader combines empathy with action, providing solutions grounded in clinical and organizational best practices.

Striking this balance begins with recognizing that your role extends beyond individual interactions. While empathy is essential for team morale, competence ensures the safety and effectiveness of patient care. By modeling this balance, you set an example for your team to follow.

Case Study: During a particularly stressful week, a nurse manager, Jessica, noticed increased tension among her team. She held a team meeting where she acknowledged their frustrations, provided emotional support, and then introduced evidence-based workflow adjustments to reduce their workload. This approach strengthened team cohesion while addressing operational challenges.

Building Credibility Through Clinical Expertise

Credibility is the backbone of effective leadership. In nursing, this often stems from your clinical knowledge and ability to guide your team in decision-making. Staying current in your field, attending professional development opportunities, and seeking certifications are key ways to maintain and build credibility.

Think of a time when your clinical expertise enhanced your leadership. How did your knowledge contribute to the team's success or patient outcomes? Leading by example is essential. When leaders demonstrate their clinical skills during high-pressure situations, they reinforce their credibility and earn their team's trust. For example, assisting with a complex patient case not only provides immediate support but also showcases your ability to empathize with and support your team.

Actionable Tool: Develop a personal learning plan. Identify one area of clinical knowledge you'd like to improve. Set specific goals, such as attending a workshop or obtaining a certification, and create a timeline to achieve them.

Clinical Judgment: The Bedrock of Leadership

While policies and guidelines serve as essential frameworks for clinical practice, they are not a substitute for critical thinking and sound judgment. Every patient and scenario are unique, and relying solely on written rules can lead to rigid decision-making that may not always align with the best outcomes. As a leader, your role includes fostering a culture where clinical judgment complements existing protocols.

Policies provide safety and consistency, but they cannot account for every nuance. Consider a nurse caring for a patient whose condition requires deviation from a standard protocol. In such situations, clinical judgment (grounded in experience and evidence) becomes crucial. Leaders must empower their teams to think critically and apply policies as tools rather than absolutes.

Encouraging this mindset involves training and trust. Leaders can model clinical judgment by discussing real-world scenarios with their teams, demonstrating how they weigh options and make decisions that prioritize patient safety while respecting organizational policies. This approach not only reinforces the importance of judgment but also builds confidence in the team's ability to make sound decisions.

Expanded Insight: Think about a time when a policy didn't perfectly fit a situation. How did clinical judgment guide the outcome? What steps did you take to ensure patient safety while maintaining team confidence and buy-in?

The Power of Evidence-Based Leadership

Evidence-based practice (EBP) ensures that your decisions are grounded in research and data. This approach not only improves patient outcomes but also enhances your credibility as a leader. Teams are more likely to trust and follow a leader whose decisions are supported by evidence rather than intuition alone.

Integrating EBP into your leadership requires a structured approach:

- Identify Opportunities: Look for areas where current practices could be improved.
- Research Solutions: Seek out studies, guidelines, or expert opinions to inform your decisions.
- Implement and Evaluate: Work with your team to apply changes and measure their impact.

The Importance of Rounding

Rounding is a vital leadership practice that connects you directly with your team and patients. As a leader, rounding allows you to:

- Build Trust: Regular check-ins demonstrate your visibility and availability, fostering trust among staff.
- Gather Insights: Observing workflows and engaging with your team helps identify

challenges, inefficiencies, or morale issues early.

- <u>Demonstrate Support</u>: By being present on the floor, you show your team that you value their work and are invested in their success.

Rounding is more than basic observation, it's about engagement. Leaders who round with purpose ask questions, provide feedback, and follow up on identified concerns. This proactive approach strengthens team morale, enhances patient outcomes, and reinforces your leadership presence.

Actionable Tool: Develop a rounding schedule that includes focused themes, such as patient safety, workflow improvements, or staff well-being. Use each round as an opportunity to gather actionable feedback and build stronger connections with your team.

Empathy in Leadership: Bridging the Gap

In a similar essence, empathy in leadership is not just about listening, it's about taking meaningful action to inspire loyalty and build trust within your team. Effective leaders ensure their team feels heard and valued by actively engaging in conversations and acknowledging the unique challenges their staff face. However, empathy becomes most impactful when it is paired with practical solutions. Recognizing struggles is important, but addressing them shows your commitment to supporting your team's well-being and success. For instance, a leader responding to staff burnout might implement a wellness initiative, such as mindfulness sessions or more flexible scheduling. These actions not only demonstrate genuine care for the team but also address operational concerns, reinforcing a balanced approach to leadership that blends compassion with action.

Leading by Example: Rolling Up Your Sleeves

One of the most effective ways to lead is to step into the trenches with your team. When leaders actively participate during challenging moments, they build trust and show solidarity. This hands-on approach not only boosts team morale but also reinforces your understanding of their daily challenges.

For instance, during a staffing shortage, a nurse leader might assist with patient care tasks, demonstrating their willingness to share the workload. These moments remind your team that you're not just a figurehead but an integral part of their success.

Compassion Meets Strategy

Leadership is about integrating compassion and strategy to drive meaningful outcomes. While empathy strengthens your team's trust and morale, strategic thinking ensures that your actions align with organizational goals. For example, by addressing team burnout with wellness initiatives doesn't just show you care, you can also reduce turnover, enhance productivity, and thus improve patient outcomes.

It was not uncommon to find myself creating a "Compassion and Strategy" checklist. For each major decision, consider how it addresses both team morale and operational goals.

Caring is only half the battle in nursing leadership. To inspire trust and achieve excellence, you must combine compassion with competence, empathy with evidence, and care with strategy. By mastering this balance, you create a leadership style that is both impactful and sustainable.

Reflection Prompts:

How do you currently balance compassion and strategy in your leadership decisions?

_____

_____

_____

_____

_____

_____

What steps can you take to strengthen your clinical expertise and credibility as a leader?

_____

_____

_____

_____

_____

_____

How can you demonstrate empathy in ways that also drive measurable outcomes?

_____

_____

_____

_____

_____

_____

Actionable Steps:

1. Identify one area in your unit where evidence-based practice can improve outcomes.

2. Plan a time to work alongside your team during a busy shift.

3. Develop a personal learning goal to enhance your clinical expertise this year.

Notes:

_____

_____

_____

_____

_____

_____

_____

_____

_____

_____

_____

_____

3

MANIFESTING YOUR INSPIRATION

The Power of Inspiration in Leadership

Leadership is as much about inspiration as it is about action. At the core of every effective leader is a personal "why"; a source of inspiration that drives their intentions and defines their approach. Whether your inspiration comes from a passion for pediatrics, a drive to achieve Magnet designation, or a commitment to improving patient outcomes, identifying and manifesting your "why" is essential. This chapter explores how leaders can discover their inspiration, channel it into their practice, and use it to create meaningful, sustainable change.

Aligning Inspiration with Leadership Intentions

Once you've identified your "why," the next step is aligning it with your leadership intentions. Your inspiration should guide not only your actions but also the culture you want to foster within your team. For example, a leader inspired by a passion for pediatrics might focus on creating a child-centered care model, ensuring that every decision prioritizes the well-being of young patients. Alternatively, a leader driven by the pursuit of Magnet designation might channel their energy into building a culture of excellence through evidence-based practice and professional development.

This alignment creates authenticity in leadership. When your actions reflect your purpose, your team will see you as genuine and motivated by more than just external expectations. Authentic leadership inspires trust and loyalty, making your team more likely to embrace your vision and goals.

Case Study: Sarah, a nurse leader in a cardiac unit, was driven by her personal experience of losing a loved one to heart disease. Her "why" became improving outcomes for cardiac patients through innovative care and team collaboration. By sharing her story and aligning her goals with this purpose, Sarah inspired her team to pursue the same level of dedication, resulting in significant improvements in patient outcomes.

Creating a Ripple Effect: Inspiration in Action

A leader's inspiration can be a tool that pioneers lasting affects across their teams. When you lead with purpose, your energy and commitment become contagious. This is known as the ripple effect: your motivation inspires others to find their own "why" and bring their best selves to their work.

To create this ripple effect, share your purpose openly with your team. Let them understand what drives you and how it shapes your decisions. Encourage them to reflect on their own motivations and align their actions with both personal and team goals. This shared sense of purpose strengthens team cohesion and fosters a culture of intentionality and excellence.

Manifesting Your Inspiration in Clinical Practice

Turning your inspiration into tangible action is the hallmark of an effective leader. This process involves weaving your "why" into every aspect of your practice, from setting goals to making decisions. For example:

- In Team Management: Use your inspiration to shape how you lead, mentor, and support your team. A leader inspired by innovation might prioritize professional career development opportunities for their staff.
- In Patient Care: Let your purpose guide patient interactions. A leader driven by compassion might model empathetic care and encourage their team to do the same.
- In Organizational Goals: Advocate for initiatives that align with your inspiration. A leader focused on quality improvement might spearhead projects that enhance care delivery or patient satisfaction.

Sustaining Your Inspiration

Even the most motivated leaders face challenges that can test their resolve. To sustain your inspiration, it's essential to nurture your "why" and reconnect with it regularly. Strategies to maintain your purpose include:

- Reflecting on Successes: Keep a journal to document moments when your leadership made a difference.
- Seeking Support: Surround yourself with mentors and colleagues who share or understand your vision.
- Celebrating Progress: Acknowledge milestones,

both personal and team-wide, to reinforce your commitment.

Leadership is a long-term journey, and staying connected to your inspiration ensures you remain grounded and focused on what truly matters.

Expanded Insight: What steps can you take to reconnect with your "why" during challenging times? How can you share this process with your team to inspire them?

Inspiration as the Heart of Leadership

Manifesting your professional inspiration means to live it daily through your actions, decisions, and interactions. By leading with authenticity and aligning your "why" with your practice, you create a leadership style that is both meaningful and impactful. As a nurse leader, your inspiration has the power to transform not only your work but also the lives of those you lead and the patients you serve.

Reflection Prompts:

What experiences in your career have shaped your "why" as a leader? How do these continue to inspire you today?

_____

_____

_____

_____

_____

_____

What challenges do you face in staying connected to your "why"? How can you address these challenges to sustain your inspiration over time?

_____

_____

_____

_____

_____

_____

How can you encourage your team to identify and act on their own sources of inspiration?

_____

_____

_____

_____

_____

_____

Actionable Steps:

1. Reflect on your "why" and write a statement that captures your leadership purpose.

2. Share your inspiration with your team and encourage them to discover their own.

3. Identify one initiative or goal that aligns with your purpose and take steps to implement it.

Notes:

_____

_____

_____

_____

_____

_____

_____

_____

_____

_____

_____

_____

_____

_____

4

PUNCTUALITY AS LEADERSHIP CURRENCY

Timeliness as a Reflection of Leadership

Punctuality is not just about being on time, it is a reflection of your reliability, professionalism, and respect for others' time. For nurse leaders, punctuality is foundational to building trust and credibility within the team. When you prioritize timeliness, you set the tone for accountability and demonstrate your commitment to the work at hand. This chapter explores why punctuality matters in leadership, how it influences team dynamics, and practical ways to incorporate timeliness into your leadership style.

Why Punctuality Matters in Leadership

Timeliness is often overlooked in leadership, yet it significantly impacts how a leader is perceived. A punctual leader communicates reliability, respect, and readiness to engage. For your team, your punctuality signals that you value their time, reinforcing their trust in your leadership. Conversely, chronic lateness can undermine your credibility and send a message of disorganization.

Punctuality also sets the tone for workplace culture. When a leader consistently starts meetings or rounds on time, it encourages the team to adopt similar habits. This creates an environment where accountability thrives, fostering efficiency and mutual respect.

Case Study: During a weekly huddle, a nurse leader consistently arrived five minutes late. Over time, the team began showing up late as well, diminishing the huddle's effectiveness. After realizing the pattern, the leader, committed to starting meetings promptly, which encouraged the team to follow suit. This small change improved overall team discipline and morale.

Punctuality as a Form of Respect

When you arrive on time, you acknowledge the importance of others' schedules and contributions. This respect fosters positive relationships within the team and builds a culture of mutual consideration. For example, when conducting performance evaluations or check-ins, punctuality demonstrates that you value the individual's time and take their concerns seriously.

Timeliness also enhances team cohesion. A leader who starts meetings on time shows respect for those who arrived punctually, discouraging late arrivals and minimizing disruptions. This creates a more organized and focused environment, allowing the team to accomplish more in less time.

Expanded Insight: Consider a time when punctuality (or the lack of it) impacted a professional interaction. What did it communicate, and how did it affect the outcome?

The Link Between Timeliness and Readiness

Punctuality is closely tied to readiness. A leader who arrives on time (and prepared) sets the stage for productive discussions and decisions. Preparation shows your team that you've put thought and effort into the task at hand, enhancing their confidence in your leadership.

For nurse leaders, readiness often extends beyond meetings to clinical or operational scenarios. Being present and prepared during a critical situation, such as an emergency department surge or a challenging patient case, reinforces your ability to lead effectively under pressure.

You may find great success in developing a pre-meeting checklist either on paper, or utilizing Microsoft OneNote to ensure you're prepared and punctual. Include items such as reviewing relevant documents, setting clear goals for the discussion, and planning your schedule to avoid last-minute delays.

Cultivating a Culture of Timeliness

As a leader, your behavior sets the tone for the entire team. By modeling punctuality, you encourage others to adopt the same habit. To cultivate this culture, consider the following strategies:

1. <u>Start and End Meetings on Time</u>: Respect everyone's schedules by adhering to set timeframes.

2. Communicate Expectations: Clearly outline the importance of punctuality to your team.
3. Provide Gentle Reminders: Encourage timeliness with friendly prompts, such as reminders about meeting start times.

When punctuality becomes part of the team's culture, it enhances productivity and reduces unnecessary stress caused by delays or poor time management.

Life Happens: Handling Unavoidable Delays

Even the most punctual leaders face unavoidable delays. In these situations, transparency and communication are essential. Informing your team about the delay and adjusting plans accordingly demonstrates professionalism and respect for their time. Avoid making lateness a pattern by reassessing your schedule and identifying ways to minimize disruptions.

Expanded Insight: How do you handle situations where delays are unavoidable? What strategies can you implement to ensure such occurrences are minimized?

Punctuality as a Leadership Asset

Punctuality is a simple yet powerful leadership trait. By prioritizing timeliness, you communicate respect, reliability, and readiness, creating a culture of accountability within your team. More than just a habit, punctuality becomes a leadership currency that strengthens trust and enhances organizational efficiency.

Reflection Prompts:

How does your punctuality (or lack thereof) impact your team's perception of you as a leader?

_____

_____

_____

_____

_____

_____

What steps can you take to improve your timeliness in both meetings and clinical settings?

_____

_____

_____

_____

_____

_____

How can you foster a culture of punctuality within your team?

_____

_____

_____

_____

_____

_____

Actionable Steps:

1. Evaluate your schedule and identify patterns of lateness to address.

2. Create a punctuality checklist to prepare for meetings and rounds.

3. Discuss the importance of timeliness with your team and set clear expectations.

Notes:

_____

_____

_____

_____

_____

_____

_____

_____

_____

_____

_____

_____

_____

5

THE POWER OF PROMPT ACTION IN LEADERSHIP

Acting with Purpose

In the fast-paced world of healthcare, hesitation can lead to missed opportunities, prolonged uncertainty, or even compromised outcomes. As a nurse leader, the ability to act promptly and with purpose is a critical skill. Prompt action demonstrates confidence, instills trust in your team, and ensures that situations are addressed efficiently and effectively. This chapter explores the balance between urgency and thoughtfulness in leadership, offering strategies to make timely decisions without sacrificing quality.

Promptness as a Leadership Strength

Promptness in leadership is about knowing when and how to act decisively. In high-stakes environments like healthcare, delays can escalate problems, while timely interventions can set a positive course. Leaders who act promptly:

- <u>Provide Clarity</u>: Prompt decisions reduce

uncertainty, helping teams focus on implementation rather than lingering on ambiguity.

- Build Trust: Teams respect leaders who step in decisively during moments of uncertainty or crisis.
- Drive Progress: Timely action keeps initiatives moving forward and prevents stagnation.

For example, during a staffing crisis, a nurse leader who quickly mobilizes resources and communicates a clear plan demonstrates their ability to lead effectively under pressure. This instills confidence in the team and prevents chaos from taking root.

Expanded Insight: Think about a time when you made a timely decision as a nurse or leader. How did it impact the outcome? What did you learn from the experience?

Balancing Urgency with Strategy

What prompt action does not mean is to act rashly. Effective leaders balance urgency with careful consideration, ensuring their decisions are both timely and strategic. This involves:

1. Assessing the Situation: Gather enough information to make an informed decision without overanalyzing.
2. Prioritizing Actions: Determine which tasks or issues require immediate attention and which can wait.

3. Delegating Responsibly: When time is of the essence, entrust team members with tasks that align with their strengths.

For example, during a sudden patient surge, a nurse leader might delegate specific roles to senior nurses while quickly coordinating additional staffing. This approach ensures that urgent needs are met while maintaining strategic oversight.

Promptness in Communication

Timely communication is a hallmark of effective leadership. Leaders who communicate promptly foster transparency and build trust, especially in moments of uncertainty. Whether it's addressing team concerns, providing updates during a crisis, or offering constructive feedback, timely communication ensures that issues are resolved before they escalate.

Consider a scenario where a team member voices frustration about staffing schedules. A leader who responds promptly while acknowledging the concern and initiating steps to address it, demonstrates their commitment to resolving issues. Delayed communication, on the other hand, can breed resentment and erode trust.

Expanded Insight: How does your current approach to communication reflect promptness? What changes could enhance your ability to address team concerns more effectively?

Leading in the Moment: Acting Decisively

Decisive leadership is particularly important in healthcare, where situations often evolve rapidly. Acting in the moment requires confidence, situational awareness, and a clear understanding of priorities. Leaders who excel at prompt action are able to:

- Trust Their Instincts: In familiar scenarios, rely on your experience to guide immediate decisions.
- Adapt Quickly: Be prepared to shift strategies as new information arises.
- Take Responsibility: Own the outcomes of your decisions, whether they succeed or require adjustment.

Overcoming Barriers to Prompt Action

Hesitation in leadership often stems from fear of failure or a desire for perfection. While caution has its place, excessive deliberation can hinder progress. To overcome these barriers:

1. Embrace Imperfection: Understand that no decision is perfect and that adjustments can be made as needed.
2. Rely on Your Team: Seek input from trusted colleagues to fill gaps in knowledge or perspective.
3. Practice Confidence: Regularly reflect on past successes to reinforce your ability to act decisively.

Actionable Tool: Keep a "Quick Decisions Journal." Document situations where you made prompt decisions, noting the outcomes and lessons learned. Over time, this practice can help build confidence in your ability to lead decisively.

The Impact of Prompt Action

The power of prompt action lies in its ability to drive progress, build trust, and inspire confidence. As a nurse leader, your ability to act decisively can set the tone for your team, ensuring that challenges are met with clarity and purpose. By balancing urgency with strategy and embracing the responsibility of decision-making, you create a leadership style that thrives under pressure.

Reflection Prompts:

How do you balance urgency with careful decision-making in your current role?

_____

_____

_____

_____

_____

_____

What situations make you hesitant to act promptly, and how can you address these barriers?

_____

_____

_____

_____

_____

_____

How does your promptness (or lack thereof) impact your team's trust and confidence in your leadership?

_____

_____

_____

_____

_____

_____

Actionable Steps:

1. Practice using a decision-making framework to improve your speed and accuracy during high-pressure scenarios.

2. Identify one area where your team would benefit from more timely communication and implement changes.

3. Reflect on a recent leadership challenge and evaluate how prompt action influenced the outcome.

Notes:

_____

_____

_____

_____

_____

_____

_____

_____

_____

_____

_____

6

KNOWING YOUR RESOURCES

Leadership Through Connection

No leader succeeds alone. The most effective nurse leaders recognize that their success lies in understanding, leveraging, and maximizing the resources available to them. Whether it's a mentor's wisdom, a colleague's expertise, or an organizational tool, knowing your resources allows you to address challenges with confidence and make informed decisions. This chapter explores how to identify and utilize resources to enhance your leadership and support your team.

Identifying Personal and Professional Resources

As a leader, it's important to evaluate the tools and networks already at your disposal. These can include:

- <u>People</u>: Mentors, colleagues, administrative staff, and interdisciplinary teams who bring diverse expertise to the table.
- <u>Knowledge</u>: Clinical guidelines, continuing education opportunities, research publications, and institutional policies.

- <u>Technology and Tools</u>: Software for scheduling, patient care dashboards, and performance tracking systems that streamline workflows.

The key is not just knowing these resources exist, but understanding how to access and apply them effectively. Start by mapping out your network and the organizational supports available to you. For example, who in your hospital is your go-to for troubleshooting staffing issues, or where can you access the latest evidence-based practices?

Actionable Tool: Create a "Resource Map" in Microsoft Excel or Google Sheets. Start by listing the people, tools, and programs available in your organization. Update it regularly as you discover new resources.

Leveraging Your Team's Strengths

One of your most valuable resources as a leader is your team. Every individual brings unique skills, knowledge, and perspectives that can complement your own. Effective leaders recognize these strengths and assign responsibilities accordingly.

For instance, a team member with strong organizational skills might excel in managing schedules, while another with a passion for education could lead in-service training sessions. By delegating tasks that align with their strengths, you empower your team, create opportunities for growth, and free yourself to focus on higher-level leadership tasks.

The Importance of Mentorship

Mentors are invaluable resources for any leader. A trusted mentor can provide guidance, offer perspective, and serve as a sounding board for difficult decisions. If you don't already have a mentor, consider seeking one within your organization or professional network.

As a leader, you can also become a mentor. Guiding others not only supports their growth but also reinforces your leadership capabilities. Mentorship creates a cycle of learning and development that benefits both parties and strengthens the overall team.

Actionable Tool: Identify a mentor or mentee and set clear goals for your relationship. For example, schedule monthly check-ins to discuss challenges, opportunities, and career development.

Building Relationships Across Departments

Leadership in nursing extends beyond your immediate team. Building relationships with colleagues in other departments or disciplines can open doors to new resources and collaborative opportunities.

For example, a strong connection with the pharmacy department can streamline medication protocols, while collaboration with IT can enhance the use of technology in your unit. These relationships not only expand your resource network but also foster a sense of unity across the organization.

Staying Resourceful in the Face of Challenges

Challenges are inevitable in leadership, but resourceful leaders use obstacles as opportunities to innovate. Whether it's a sudden policy change or an unexpected staffing issue, take a step back, assess your resources, and involve your team in problem-solving.

For example, during the early days of the COVID-19 pandemic, nurse leaders had to adapt rapidly, often with limited resources. Those who excelled were the ones who communicated openly, sought out creative solutions, and leaned on their networks for support.

In moments of crisis, use the following framework:
1. Assess the challenge.
2. Identify available resources (people, tools, knowledge).
3. Develop a short-term and long-term action plan.
4. Reflect on the outcome and adjust your resource strategy as needed.

Empowering Leadership Through Resources

One of the most misconstrued assumptions about leadership is that one must have all the answers. The reality is that the true value lies in knowing where to find answers and whom to rely on. By identifying, leveraging, and building resources, you create a strong foundation for yourself and your team. Effective use of resources not only enhances your ability to lead but also fosters a culture of collaboration and continuous improvement.

Reflection Prompts:

What are the top three resources you currently rely on as a leader?

_____

_____

_____

_____

_____

_____

Are there underutilized resources in your organization that could benefit your team?

_____

_____

_____

_____

_____

_____

How can you strengthen your relationships with key individuals or departments to expand your resource network?

_____

_____

_____

_____

_____

Actionable Steps:

1. Update your "Resource Map" with new contacts or tools.

2. Identify one team member's strength and delegate a task that aligns with it this week.

3. Reach out to a colleague in another department to discuss potential collaborative opportunities.

Notes:

_____

_____

_____

_____

_____

_____

_____

_____

_____

_____

_____

Part II: Navigating Leadership Transitions

7

FROM COWORKER TO MANAGER: LEADING FORMER PEERS

A Unique Transition

Becoming a manager for the team you once worked alongside can be one of the most challenging transitions in leadership. The relationships built as peers, defined by camaraderie, and shared struggles, now shift into a dynamic where authority and accountability must take center stage. While the trust you've already built with your former coworkers is a strength, navigating this transition requires clear communication, emotional intelligence, and a firm understanding of your new responsibilities.

Confronting the Dynamics of Role Change

Transitioning from coworker to manager of your former peers inherently changes the relationships you once shared. What may have been casual conversations in the breakroom can now carry a different weight when viewed through the lens of authority. Acknowledging this shift and addressing it openly is essential. As a leader, you're no longer just a teammate, you're a decision-maker and the person responsible for ensuring the team's success.

This shift often requires confronting conflict with those who may question your decisions or find it hard to separate the past from your current role. It's important to address these situations directly but tactfully. Acknowledging the awkwardness of the transition with honesty can often diffuse tension. For example, you might say, "I understand this is an adjustment for all of us, but I'm committed to doing what's best for the team and ensuring we're successful together."

While maintaining empathy is vital, it's equally important to establish that your role as a manager includes representing organizational priorities, even when they conflict with personal relationships or staff preferences. Striking this balance is challenging but necessary to be effective in your position.

Balancing Staff Favor with Operational Demands

One of the most complex aspects of any transition is balancing the desire to maintain the favor and sympathy of your former peers with the operational and business aspects of your role. As a manager, you are tasked with not only supporting your team but also ensuring that the unit meets organizational goals, such as productivity, budget management, and compliance with policies.

However, it's equally important to stand by and defend your team when their interests are not being considered. Leadership isn't about simply enforcing directives, it's about being an advocate who bridges the gap between staff and organizational priorities. For instance, if a policy disproportionately affects your team, it's your role to communicate their concerns and seek adjustments where appropriate. Defending your team not only builds trust but also reinforces your commitment to their well-being.

It's critical to communicate transparently with your team about your dual role. For example, when implementing a new policy that may initially seem burdensome, frame it in terms of how it aligns with broader objectives, such as improving patient care or streamlining workflows. This approach helps your team see that your decisions are not personal but are guided by a bigger picture, even as you continue to represent their best interests.

Case Study: Maria, a newly promoted nurse manager, struggled to balance her friendships with former coworkers while enforcing stricter scheduling protocols. By explaining how the new approach would reduce burnout and improve patient outcomes, she earned her team's understanding, even if the change wasn't immediately popular.

Establishing Professional Boundaries

Setting boundaries is critical to maintaining respect and authority in your new role. This doesn't mean abandoning camaraderie or connection but rather redefining relationships in a way that supports mutual trust and professionalism.

For example, casual venting sessions with former peers may now be inappropriate, as they can blur the lines between personal and professional. Instead, create structured opportunities for open dialogue, such as team meetings or one-on-one check-ins, where concerns can be addressed constructively. Boundaries also extend to maintaining impartiality. Favoritism, whether real or perceived, can erode team morale and undermine your credibility as a leader.

Fostering a Collaborative Environment

While the transition to manager requires asserting authority, it also provides an opportunity to foster collaboration. Use your insider knowledge of the team to empower individuals and promote a sense of shared ownership over outcomes. Seek input on decisions when appropriate and highlight team contributions to create a culture of mutual respect and trust.

Actionable Tool: Develop a communication plan that includes regular check-ins with team members to gather feedback, discuss challenges, and celebrate successes.

Redefining Relationships for Leadership Success

The transition from coworker to manager is one that requires self-awareness, transparency, and a focus on the broader goals of the team and organization. By addressing the dynamics of role change, balancing empathy with operational demands, and fostering a collaborative environment, you can navigate this transition successfully and build a foundation of trust and respect.

Reflection Prompts:

How have your relationships with former peers changed since becoming their manager, and how have you addressed these changes?

_____

_____

_____

_____

_____

_____

How do you currently balance representing your team's needs with the operational goals of your organization?

_____

_____

_____

_____

_____

_____

What steps can you take to establish or reinforce professional boundaries with your team?

_____

_____

_____

_____

_____

Actionable Steps:

1. Schedule a meeting with your team to openly discuss the transition and set expectations for your role as manager.

2. Identify one area where operational goals and team needs overlap, and create a plan to communicate this alignment to your team.

3. Establish a routine for individual check-ins to strengthen professional relationships and address concerns constructively.

Notes:

_____

_____

_____

_____

_____

_____

_____

_____

_____

_____

_____

_____

_____

8

SETTING BOUNDARIES WITHOUT BURNING BRIDGES

The Art of Balance

Leadership often feels like a delicate balancing act. You must manage team and stakeholder relationships alongside meeting responsibilities, all while safeguarding your own well-being. As a leader, the ability to set boundaries is crucial not only for protecting your mental health but also for fostering trust and respect within your team. However, setting boundaries is not about saying "no" indiscriminately or distancing yourself from your team. It's about creating clear, respectful limits that allow you to maintain effectiveness and accountability without sacrificing relationships or morale. This chapter explores strategies for setting boundaries that protect both your leadership role and your connections with others.

Why Boundaries Matter in Leadership

Boundaries are essential for preventing burnout and maintaining clarity in your role. Leaders who fail to set boundaries often find themselves overwhelmed, constantly overcommitting, and struggling to fulfill their obligations. Clear boundaries establish expectations for how time, communication, and responsibilities are managed, creating an environment of mutual respect and efficiency.

For example, imagine a leader who answers emails late into the night or takes on every task themselves to avoid burdening their team. Over time, this lack of boundaries can erode their capacity to lead effectively and diminish the team's trust in their decisions. By setting limits on when and how you're accessible, you model healthy work habits and demonstrate respect for your own and others' time.

Communicating Boundaries Effectively

The success of boundary-setting lies in communication. Clearly articulating your limits ensures your team understands them and views them as a positive framework rather than a restriction. Start by framing boundaries in terms of benefits to the team. For example, instead of saying, "I won't answer emails after hours," you might explain, "I'll respond to emails during working hours so I can fully focus on urgent issues when they arise."

When communicating boundaries, consistency is key. Enforcing them regularly reinforces their importance and reduces confusion. If your team sees you occasionally breaking your own boundaries, they may perceive them as flexible, leading to misunderstandings or even resentment.

Case Study: A nurse leader consistently held open-door hours during specified times each week. By adhering to this schedule, the leader ensured their team had regular access for discussions while preserving uninterrupted time for administrative tasks. This approach fostered trust and organization without creating unnecessary barriers.

Saying No Without Damaging Relationships

One of the hardest aspects of setting boundaries is learning to say "no." As a leader, you may feel compelled to take on every task or request to demonstrate your commitment. However, saying "yes" to everything can quickly lead to overextension and inefficiency.

Saying "no" effectively involves framing it as a positive decision. For example, if a team member asks for additional resources during a busy period, you might respond with, "I understand this is important, but given our current priorities, we'll need to revisit this request next month." This approach acknowledges their needs while maintaining focus on current goals.

Expanded Insight: Think of a time when you struggled to say "no" to a request. What was the impact on your workload and team dynamics? How might a different response have improved the situation?

Protecting Personal Time While Leading

Leadership can often blur the boundaries between professional and personal time, particularly in high-demand roles. Protecting your personal time is vital for maintaining your energy and enthusiasm for leadership. Setting firm limits, such as designated days off or specific hours for responding to emails, ensures you have the opportunity to recharge.

This isn't about neglecting your responsibilities; it's about showing your team that self-care is a priority. By modeling work-life balance, you empower your team to do the same, creating a healthier and more sustainable workplace culture.

Actionable Tool: Create a weekly schedule that includes "non-negotiable" personal time blocks. Share this schedule with your team so they know when you're unavailable and can plan accordingly.

Boundaries Build Stronger Bridges

Far from being a barrier, boundaries create structure, clarity, and respect within a team. By setting and communicating your limits, you establish a leadership style that protects your well-being, fosters trust, and encourages mutual accountability. When done thoughtfully, setting boundaries strengthens relationships, ensuring that you can lead effectively without compromising your personal or professional values.

Reflection Prompts:

How do you currently set boundaries in your leadership role, and how effective are they?

_____

_____

_____

_____

_____

_____

What is one boundary you've struggled to enforce, and what steps can you take to communicate it more effectively?

_____

_____

_____

_____

_____

_____

How does your approach to boundaries influence your team's perception of work-life balance?

_____

_____

_____

_____

_____

_____

Actionable Steps:

1. Identify one area where a lack of boundaries is impacting your effectiveness and create a plan to address it.

2. Communicate one new boundary to your team this week, framing it in terms of mutual benefits.

3. Schedule a "boundary check-in" with yourself every month to reflect on and adjust your limits as needed.

Notes:

_____

_____

_____

_____

_____

_____

_____

_____

_____

_____

_____

_____

_____

_____

9

THE POWER OF SILENCE: LISTEN TO LEAD

Silence as a Leadership Tool

In a world where quick responses and constant communication are often seen as marks of competence, the power of silence is frequently overlooked. However, silence can be one of the most impactful tools in a leader's repertoire. It fosters deep listening, encourages reflection, and creates space for others to contribute. For nurse leaders, mastering the art of silence is essential for building trust, enhancing team communication, and making thoughtful decisions. This chapter explores how silence can transform leadership and offers strategies for integrating it into your daily interactions.

The Role of Silence in Leadership

Silence is not the absence of communication, it is a valuable form of communication in itself. It conveys attentiveness, respect, and a willingness to hear others out. When leaders practice intentional silence, they create a safe space for their team members to express themselves. This is especially important in nursing, where emotions often run high, and team dynamics can be complex.

For example, during a team meeting, a leader who allows a moment of silence after asking a question invites more thoughtful responses. The pause gives team members the time to reflect and articulate their thoughts without feeling rushed. This practice not only enhances the quality of discussion but also shows that the leader values their input.

Listening Beyond Words

Silence goes hand in hand with active listening, a skill that involves more than just hearing words. Active listening requires leaders to pay attention to tone, body language, and underlying emotions. These nonverbal cues often reveal insights that words alone cannot.

Consider a situation where a team member expresses frustration about scheduling but hesitates to elaborate. A leader practicing active listening might notice their tense posture or anxious tone and use silence to encourage further sharing. Rather than filling the silence with solutions or reassurances, the leader's quiet presence can signal empathy and an openness to understanding the deeper issue.

Case Study: During a one-on-one conversation, a nurse expressed concern about burnout but downplayed their feelings. The leader resisted the urge to immediately respond and instead maintained a moment of silence, followed by an open-ended question: "Can you tell me more about what's been on your mind lately?" This approach allowed the nurse to share more honestly, leading to a productive discussion about workload adjustments and support systems.

When Silence Speaks Louder Than Words

There are moments when silence is more powerful than any words you could offer. These include situations of heightened emotion, such as conflicts or grief, where immediate responses might be counterproductive. In these moments, silence can demonstrate empathy and give others the time they need to process their emotions.

For instance, if a team member becomes visibly upset during a discussion, pausing to let them gather their thoughts rather than rushing to resolve the situation shows respect for their emotional state. Similarly, silence during a difficult decision-making process can convey the gravity of the situation and allow all voices to be heard before action is taken.

Expanded Insight: Think about a recent situation where silence might have been a more effective response than speaking. How could you apply this lesson in future interactions?

Silence as a Decision-Making Strategy

In leadership, silence is a valuable tool for processing information and considering options before making decisions. While speaking immediately can sometimes convey confidence, rushing to conclusions without adequate reflection often leads to mistakes. Silence gives leaders the time to weigh perspectives, analyze data, and approach decisions thoughtfully.

For the clinical setting, an example could look like when a policy review meeting happens, a nurse leader might encounter differing opinions from the team. By pausing to consider each viewpoint (or even refrain from making a decision until after the meeting) rather than responding impulsively, the leader can make a more informed and balanced decision. This approach not only improves outcomes but also models thoughtful leadership for the team. You do not want to rush to have

Creating Space for Team Voices

One of the most significant benefits of silence in leadership is its ability to create space for others to speak. When leaders dominate conversations, they inadvertently stifle creativity and discourage participation. Intentional silence, on the other hand, invites collaboration and empowers team members to share their ideas.

In team settings, a leader might pose a question and then remain silent, resisting the urge to fill the pause. This creates an opening for others to contribute and often leads to more innovative solutions. By stepping back, the leader shifts the focus from themselves to the collective intelligence of the group.

Actionable Tool: Practice a "silent pause" in your next team meeting. After asking a question, wait at least 10 seconds before speaking again. Observe how this pause impacts the quality and quantity of responses.

Overcoming the Discomfort of Silence

For many leaders, silence can feel uncomfortable or even awkward. This discomfort often stems from a cultural emphasis on constant communication and immediate solutions. In nursing, this challenge is compounded by a professional mindset that trains nurses to provide immediate answers and solve problems quickly, even when they may not have all the necessary information. While this approach is critical in clinical situations, it can be detrimental in leadership roles.

New leaders may feel compelled to speak up or offer solutions immediately to project confidence and control. However, rushing to address a problem without fully assessing the situation can convey oversimplification or even incompetence. It's important to recognize that taking time to gather input and evaluate options demonstrates thoughtfulness and strategic decision-making, which builds trust in your leadership.

This process may take days, requiring input from various team members or external resources, but the patience and discipline to wait are invaluable. Leaders who utilize silence to reflect, listen, and research options model a measured approach that inspires confidence. By resisting the urge to fill every pause with premature solutions, you show your team that you value accuracy, depth, and collaboration over quick fixes.

Case Study: A new manager initially struggled with the silence that followed tough feedback discussions. Over time, they learned to embrace these pauses, recognizing that silence allowed team members to process feedback and respond constructively. This change improved the quality of their interactions and strengthened team relationships.

The Transformative Power of Silence

Silence is a simple yet profound leadership tool. By listening deeply, creating space for reflection, and resisting the urge to fill every pause, nurse leaders can foster trust, enhance communication, and make more thoughtful decisions. In a fast-paced and demanding environment, the power of silence offers a counterbalance, reminding us that sometimes, the most impactful action is to say nothing at all.

Reflection Prompts:

How comfortable are you with using silence in your leadership interactions, and what situations make it challenging?

_____

_____

_____

_____

_____

_____

When was the last time you practiced active listening during a conversation? How did silence contribute to that experience?

_____

_____

_____

_____

_____

_____

What steps can you take to create more intentional moments of silence in your daily leadership practices?

_____

_____

_____

_____

_____

Actionable Steps:

1. Incorporate a 10-second silent pause during your next team meeting or discussion.

2. Practice active listening by focusing on nonverbal cues during one-on-one conversations.

3. Identify one leadership scenario where silence could enhance your response and commit to using it this week.

Notes:

_____

_____

_____

_____

_____

_____

_____

_____

_____

_____

_____

_____

_____

10

DRAWING THE LINE: BALANCING EMPATHY WITH OBJECTIVITY

The Delicate Balance

Empathy is at the heart of nursing and a key component of effective leadership. It allows leaders to connect with their team, understand their challenges, and foster trust. However, in leadership, there is a fine line between being empathetic and losing objectivity. Overidentifying with your team's struggles or allowing emotions to cloud your judgment can lead to inconsistencies, favoritism, or difficulty making tough decisions. This chapter explores how to balance empathy with objectivity, ensuring that leaders support their teams while maintaining fairness and integrity.

Empathy as a Leadership Foundation

Empathy enables leaders to build genuine relationships with their teams. It involves active listening, understanding perspectives, and offering support during difficult times. Empathy creates an environment of psychological safety, where team members feel valued and understood.

However, empathy alone isn't enough. While it strengthens connections, it can also lead to blurred boundaries if not tempered with objectivity. For example, a leader who consistently sides with their team in conflicts without considering the broader organizational context risks undermining their credibility.

Empathy becomes most effective when paired with fairness and a commitment to impartiality. Leaders must strive to balance emotional support with an objective assessment of situations, ensuring that all team members are treated equally.

The Risks of Overidentifying

Overidentifying with your team's struggles can make it difficult to enforce rules, address conflicts, or make decisions that might not align with everyone's preferences. Leaders who focus too heavily on empathy may inadvertently foster an environment where accountability is compromised.

For instance, a leader who avoids addressing a team member's repeated lateness out of empathy for their personal challenges may unintentionally create resentment among other team members who adhere to the rules. Similarly, over-empathizing with one group during a disagreement can lead to perceptions of favoritism, eroding trust within the team.

To avoid these pitfalls, it's important to maintain a clear perspective and approach each situation with a balance of compassion and objectivity.

Case Study: A nurse leader encountered a conflict between two staff members, one of whom was a close colleague from their days as a bedside nurse. Recognizing their potential bias, the leader sought input from a neutral third party before making a decision, ensuring fairness and maintaining team trust.

Strategies for Balancing Empathy & Objectivity

- Pausing Before Responding: When faced with emotionally charged situations, take a moment to reflect before responding. This pause allows you to assess the situation objectively and determine the best course of action.
- Seek Multiple Perspectives: Gather input from all parties involved before making decisions. This ensures that you're considering diverse viewpoints and avoiding favoritism.
- Focus on Facts, Not Feelings: While it's important to acknowledge emotions, base your decisions on objective data and evidence. For example, if addressing a performance issue, focus on measurable outcomes rather than subjective impressions.
- Setting Clear Expectations: Communicate your expectations for behavior, performance, and accountability clearly and consistently. This reduces ambiguity and ensures fairness in how team members are treated.

Empathy in Tough Decisions

Balancing empathy with objectivity doesn't mean abandoning compassion during difficult decisions.

Instead, it's about approaching these situations with transparency and fairness while showing understanding for how decisions may impact your team.

For example, if you must reassign a nurse to a less favorable shift due to staffing shortages, acknowledge their disappointment while explaining the rationale behind the decision. Offering support, such as discussing future scheduling adjustments or resources to help them adapt, demonstrates empathy without compromising the operational needs of the unit.

Leading with Compassion and Integrity

Balancing empathy with objectivity is one of the most challenging aspects of leadership, but it's also one of the most rewarding. Leaders who master this balance create environments of trust, fairness, and accountability. By supporting your team emotionally while maintaining a clear and unbiased perspective, you demonstrate both compassion and integrity, setting the foundation for a strong and cohesive team.

Reflection Prompts:

How do you currently balance empathy and objectivity in your leadership decisions?

_____

_____

_____

_____

_____

_____

Think of a situation where over-empathizing impacted your ability to lead effectively. What could you do differently in a similar scenario?

_____

_____

_____

_____

_____

_____

How can you ensure that your decisions are perceived as fair and unbiased by your team?

_____

_____

_____

_____

_____

_____

Actionable Steps:

1. Identify one area where emotions may be influencing your objectivity and create a plan to address it.

2. Practice pausing before responding during your next challenging interaction to reflect on the balance between empathy and fairness.

3. Develop a checklist for decision-making that includes gathering multiple perspectives and focusing on measurable facts.

Notes:

Part III: Empowering Teams

11

HIRING FOR COMPLEMENTARY STRENGTHS: TRUSTING YOUR TEAM'S EXPERTISE

Building a Balanced Team

Another essential yet challenging responsibility of a leader is hiring the right people. As a nurse leader, your team's success depends not only on each individual's competence but also on how their skills complement one another. Effective hiring requires a mindset shift: rather than seeking individuals who mirror your strengths, focus on building a diverse team where each member fills gaps in expertise and brings unique value. This chapter explores strategies for identifying complementary strengths during the hiring process, trusting your team's expertise, and fostering a culture of collaboration.

Recognizing Your Own Leadership Gaps

The first step in hiring for complementary strengths is understanding your own areas of weakness. As a leader, self-awareness is critical, not only for personal growth but also for building a well-rounded team. Acknowledging that you don't have to know or do everything is liberating and creates an opportunity to leverage others' talents.

For example, if you're a visionary leader who excels at big-picture planning but struggles with details, hiring a team member with strong organizational skills can help ensure that nothing falls through the cracks. Similarly, if you find communication challenging, bringing on someone who is naturally adept at interpersonal relationships can enhance your team's cohesion and morale.

Actionable Tool: Conduct a personal leadership audit. Identify three areas where you feel less confident or capable, and prioritize hiring individuals who can strengthen these areas.

Evaluating Candidates for Complementary Strengths

The hiring process should go beyond assessing technical skills and clinical expertise. While these are important, it's equally critical to evaluate candidates' interpersonal skills, problem-solving abilities, and how they align with the team's existing dynamics.

During interviews, ask behavioral questions that reveal how candidates handle challenges and collaborate with others. For example, "Can you describe a time when you worked on a team with individuals who had very different approaches or personalities? How did you navigate that dynamic?" This question can help you gauge whether a candidate will bring valuable diversity of thought to your team.

It's also helpful to involve your current team in the hiring process. Allowing team members to meet candidates and provide feedback can offer additional perspectives on how well a candidate's strengths align with the team's needs.

Trusting Your Team's Expertise

Hiring individuals with complementary strengths is only the first step; the real challenge lies in trusting their expertise and empowering them to take ownership of their roles. Micromanaging or second-guessing your team's decisions not only undermines their confidence but also stifles creativity and growth.

As a leader, your role is to set clear expectations, provide support, and then step back to let your team shine. Trusting your team doesn't mean abandoning oversight; it means creating an environment where they feel confident making decisions and know you're there as a safety net if needed.

Expanded Insight: How comfortable are you with delegating responsibilities to team members? What steps can you take to build greater trust in their expertise?

Encouraging Collaboration Among Diverse Strengths

A diverse team thrives when its members' strengths are not only recognized but also actively leveraged through collaboration. Leaders can facilitate this by creating opportunities for team members to share their skills and learn from one another.

For example, pairing a nurse with strong clinical expertise but limited technological skills with a colleague proficient in electronic health records fosters mutual growth. Similarly, encouraging team members to participate in cross-functional projects can help them develop new competencies while contributing their unique strengths. This could be tied into a clinical ladder project if already in place within your workplace. It could even be profit sharing criteria for a team to meet at year-end bonus distributions.

Avoiding Common Pitfalls in Hiring and Team Development

While hiring for complementary strengths is crucial, there are common pitfalls leaders should avoid:

- Overemphasizing Fit: While it's important for candidates to align with the team culture, over-prioritizing "fit" can lead to homogeneity and limit diverse perspectives.
- Ignoring Potential: Don't overlook candidates with less experience but high potential for growth and adaptability.
- Failing to Address Skill Gaps: If a critical skill is missing from your team, prioritize filling that gap rather than hiring someone with redundant strengths.

By being mindful of these pitfalls, you can build a team that is both dynamic and well-rounded.

Involving Unit Educators in the Hiring Process

When building a well-rounded team, it's essential to recognize that every new hire will require some form of orientation, no matter how experienced they are. Including unit educators in the hiring process ensures that candidates are evaluated not just for their technical skills and team fit, but also for their ability to adapt to the training and development processes of the unit.

Unit educators can assess whether a candidate's learning style aligns with the available onboarding resources and training timelines. For example, a candidate who thrives in structured learning environments may excel with a detailed orientation plan, while someone who prefers hands-on learning might benefit from additional mentorship opportunities. By considering these factors during interviews, educators can identify potential challenges early and recommend tailored onboarding strategies.

Involving educators also highlights the team's commitment to professional development, which can make the position more appealing to candidates. It demonstrates that the unit values growth and is prepared to invest in their success.

Case Study: A nurse manager partnered with the unit educator to interview candidates for a high-turnover position. During the interview, the educator asked specific questions about how the candidate had approached learning new skills in previous roles. This helped the team select a candidate whose learning style aligned with the unit's fast-paced orientation program, leading to a smoother transition and higher retention.

Building a Stronger Team, Together

Hiring for complementary strengths is about more than filling positions, it's about building a cohesive team that thrives on diversity of thought and expertise. By recognizing your own leadership gaps, evaluating candidates holistically, and fostering collaboration, you create an environment where every team member contributes uniquely to the group's success. Trusting your team's expertise not only empowers them but also strengthens your leadership by demonstrating confidence and humility.

Reflection Prompts:

What are your top three strengths as a leader, and how do they influence your hiring decisions?

_____

_____

_____

_____

_____

_____

How do you currently evaluate candidates for complementary strengths? What changes could you make to improve this process?

_____

_____

_____

_____

_____

_____

How do you encourage collaboration among team members with diverse skills and perspectives?

_____

_____

_____

_____

_____

_____

Actionable Steps:

1. Conduct a leadership audit to identify areas where you could benefit from complementary team strengths.

2. Develop three new interview questions designed to assess candidates' interpersonal skills and adaptability.

3. Create a team skills inventory to better leverage existing strengths and identify gaps to address in future hires.

Notes:

_____

_____

_____

_____

_____

_____

_____

_____

_____

_____

_____

_____

12

BUILDING TRUST THROUGH ACCOUNTABILITY

The Foundation of Leadership Trust

Trust is the cornerstone of effective leadership. Without it, even the most competent leaders struggle to inspire their teams or drive meaningful progress. Accountability, meanwhile, is one of the most powerful ways to build and sustain that trust. By demonstrating reliability, following through on commitments, and holding both yourself and your team to high standards, you create a culture of mutual respect and shared responsibility. This chapter delves into how accountability strengthens trust within teams, explores strategies for fostering accountability at all levels, and highlights creative approaches to reinforce these principles.

The Connection Between Accountability and Trust

Accountability, much like punctuality, can be confused with just meeting deadlines or completing tasks. The reality is that it's more about consistently delivering on promises and owning the outcomes of your actions. When leaders demonstrate accountability, they model the behaviors they expect from their team, reinforcing a culture of integrity.

For example, if a leader promises to advocate for new resources during a budget review but fails to follow through, their team may question their reliability. Conversely, when leaders take responsibility for setbacks, admit mistakes, and actively work to resolve issues, they demonstrate authenticity and commitment to the team's success.

Team members also need to feel that accountability is applied fairly and consistently. Leaders who hold everyone to the same standard foster a sense of equity, while those who overlook certain individuals' lapses risk eroding trust within the team.

Fostering a Culture of Accountability

Creating a culture of accountability requires clear expectations, consistent communication, and mutual respect. Leaders can foster this culture by:

- Setting Clear Expectations: Ensure that everyone on the team understands their roles, responsibilities, and the specific outcomes they're working toward. Clarity reduces confusion and provides a framework for evaluating performance.
- Providing Regular Feedback: Constructive feedback reinforces accountability by acknowledging strengths and identifying areas for improvement. Regular check-ins also create opportunities for team members to discuss

challenges and seek support.

- Modeling Accountability: Leaders must practice what they preach. Admitting mistakes, meeting deadlines, and honoring commitments show the team that accountability is a shared value.
- Encouraging Peer Accountability: Empower team members to hold each other accountable. For instance, a team could establish a peer-review process for projects or create shared goals that encourage collaboration and mutual responsibility.

Creative Recognition: A Tool for Accountability

Recognition is a powerful motivator for fostering accountability within a team. When team members feel that their efforts are noticed and valued, they are more likely to take ownership of their work and consistently strive for excellence. Creative recognition initiatives can reinforce accountability while simultaneously building morale and camaraderie.

For example, implementing a points-based recognition system can reward team members for meeting goals, such as completing projects on time or mentoring colleagues. These points could translate into tangible rewards like gift cards or extra time off, adding an element of fun and competition. Alternatively, a community recognition book or digital platform allows team members to write notes of appreciation for their peers, highlighting instances where accountability and teamwork shine. Reading these notes aloud during team meetings or morning huddles serves as a public acknowledgment of individual and collective efforts, fostering a sense of shared achievement. Personalized gestures, such as handwritten thank-you cards or emails, can also leave a lasting impact. For instance, recognizing a nurse who voluntarily stayed late to assist with a patient transfer reinforces the importance of going above and beyond while strengthening the bond between leader and team.

These recognition strategies not only promote accountability but also create a positive and supportive work environment where team members feel valued and inspired.

Actionable Tool: Launch a team recognition program tailored to your staff's preferences, starting with a small initiative like a digital recognition wall or thank-you notes during monthly meetings.

Addressing Accountability Challenges

Maintaining accountability within a team is not always straightforward, particularly when resistance arises or expectations are not met. Addressing these challenges requires leaders to approach situations directly yet constructively, ensuring small issues are resolved before they escalate into larger problems.

Resistance to feedback is one of the most common challenges in accountability. Team members may push back due to a lack of understanding or a perception of unfairness. Leaders can navigate this resistance by approaching conversations with empathy and focusing on behaviors rather than personal attributes. For example, instead of saying, "You're always late," a leader might say, "I noticed you've been arriving late to shifts recently. Let's discuss how we can address this together."

This approach frames the issue as a shared problem, fostering collaboration rather than defensiveness.

Accountability also involves rebuilding trust after lapses, whether the lapse occurs on the leader's part or within the team. A leader who fails to meet a commitment should openly acknowledge the mistake, outline steps for improvement, and follow through on their promises. Similarly, when addressing a team member's accountability issues, it's important to provide clear expectations and support their efforts to improve.

Leaders must balance accountability with empathy, understanding that personal struggles or resource constraints may contribute to lapses. By acknowledging these challenges and offering support (such as adjusted workloads or additional training), leaders can maintain trust while addressing the root cause of the issue.

The Long-Term Impact of Accountability

Building trust through accountability is an ongoing process that requires consistency, fairness, and a commitment to shared goals. When leaders prioritize accountability, they create a culture of reliability, respect, and high performance. This culture not only strengthens teams but also improves patient outcomes and organizational success.

Reflection Prompts:

How do you currently demonstrate accountability to your team, and where could you improve?

_____

_____

_____

_____

_____

_____

What strategies have you used to address accountability challenges, and how effective were they?

_____

_____

_____

_____

_____

_____

How can recognition be used more effectively within your team to reinforce accountability?

_____

_____

_____

_____

_____

_____

Actionable Steps:

1. Review your team's current processes and identify one area where accountability could be strengthened. Develop a plan to address it this week.

2. Implement a recognition initiative, such as a community recognition book or personalized thank-you notes, to highlight accountability.

3. Schedule a team meeting to clarify roles and expectations, ensuring everyone understands their responsibilities and goals.

Notes:

_____

_____

_____

_____

_____

_____

_____

_____

_____

_____

_____

_____

13

INTERPROFESSIONAL COLLABORATION: LEADING BEYOND NURSING

Collaboration as a Core Leadership Skill

In the complex world of healthcare, successful patient outcomes depend on the seamless collaboration of diverse professionals, including nurses, physicians, therapists, technicians, and administrators. As a nurse leader, your ability to lead beyond the nursing team and foster strong interprofessional relationships is critical to ensuring cohesive teamwork, reducing silos, and improving overall care quality. This chapter explores the unique challenges and opportunities of interprofessional collaboration, offering strategies to strengthen communication, resolve conflicts, and lead effectively across disciplines.

The Importance of Interprofessional Collaboration

Healthcare is inherently interdisciplinary. Each

professional brings a unique perspective, expertise, and skill set to the table, but these differences can also create misunderstandings or conflict. Nurse leaders are often positioned at the intersection of these diverse teams, serving as liaisons who bridge gaps and foster cohesion.

Effective interprofessional collaboration leads to better patient outcomes, fewer errors, and higher team satisfaction. For example, strong collaboration between nursing staff and physical therapists can streamline discharge planning, ensuring patients receive consistent guidance on mobility and recovery. Conversely, poor collaboration can result in duplicated efforts, communication breakdowns, and negative patient experiences.

As a leader, fostering collaboration means not only facilitating teamwork but also modeling the behaviors you want to see. By prioritizing mutual respect, clear communication, and shared goals, you create a foundation for success.

Building Relationships Across Disciplines

Leading beyond nursing begins with building relationships. Establishing trust and rapport with colleagues in other disciplines sets the tone for effective collaboration. Start by seeking opportunities to connect with team members outside of formal meetings. For example, attending physician rounds or joining interdisciplinary committees demonstrates your commitment to understanding their perspectives.

Active listening is another cornerstone of relationship-building. When team members feel heard and valued, they are more likely to engage in open and productive communication. During interdisciplinary meetings, make a point to acknowledge contributions, ask clarifying questions, and encourage input from all participants.

Case Example: A nurse leader noticed recurring friction between nurses and respiratory therapists over workflow responsibilities. By hosting a joint meeting and facilitating open dialogue, they identified overlapping tasks and restructured responsibilities to align with each discipline's strengths. The improved workflow reduced conflict and increased team efficiency.

Navigating Interprofessional Conflicts

Conflict is inevitable in any team, but it is especially common in interdisciplinary settings where differing priorities, communication styles, and cultural norms intersect. Nurse leaders must approach conflict as an opportunity for growth rather than a barrier to collaboration.

Begin by addressing conflicts early. Allowing tensions to fester can escalate misunderstandings and damage relationships. Use a structured approach, such as the *DESC model* (Describe, Express, Specify, Consequences), to guide conversations toward resolution. For example:

- Describe the issue: "I've noticed that there's been confusion about who should handle post-op mobility instructions."
- Express the impact: "This has led to delays in patient discharge."
- Specify a solution: "Let's clarify roles during the next team huddle."
- Consequences: "This will help streamline care and improve patient satisfaction."

Mediating conflicts also requires a neutral stance. Focus on shared goals, such as patient care or efficiency, and steer discussions away from blame. Leaders who remain calm, empathetic, and solutions-oriented set a positive tone for conflict resolution.

Promoting Effective Communication

Communication is the backbone of collaboration, yet interprofessional teams often face barriers such as jargon, hierarchical differences, and inconsistent messaging. Nurse leaders can overcome these challenges by promoting clarity, consistency, and inclusivity in communication.

One strategy is to standardize communication tools, such as *SBARQ* (Situation, Background, Assessment, Recommendation, Questions), to ensure concise and structured exchanges. For example, using SBARQ during interdisciplinary rounds ensures that everyone has the same understanding of a patient's status and care plan.

Leaders should also encourage open communication channels. This could involve establishing regular interdisciplinary huddles, where team members can discuss updates, raise concerns, and align priorities. Creating a safe environment where all voices are valued, regardless of role or hierarchy, fosters trust and transparency.

Leading Collaborative Initiatives

Effective nurse leaders not only facilitate collaboration but also champion initiatives that bring teams together. Collaborative projects, such as quality improvement initiatives or patient-centered care programs, provide opportunities for interdisciplinary engagement and shared ownership.

For example, a leader tasked with reducing patient fall rates might assemble a team that includes nurses, physical therapists, environmental services staff, and administrators. By aligning everyone toward a common goal and leveraging each discipline's expertise, the leader creates a sense of unity and shared accountability.

Recognize and celebrate successes along the way. Whether it's meeting a milestone in a project or improving a specific patient outcome, acknowledging contributions reinforces the value of collaboration and motivates continued teamwork.

Fostering Collaboration as a Leadership Imperative

Interprofessional collaboration is a vital skill for nurse leaders who aim to drive positive outcomes and build cohesive, high-performing teams. By cultivating relationships, resolving conflicts, and promoting effective communication, leaders can break down silos and unite professionals around shared goals. Leading within the nursing field cant just be about managing people, it requires a focus on inspiring cooperation, respect, and innovation across disciplines.

Reflection Prompts:

Reflect on a recent interdisciplinary collaboration. What worked well, and what could have been improved?

_____

_____

_____

_____

_____

_____

How can you build stronger relationships with professionals in other disciplines?

_____

_____

_____

_____

_____

_____

What steps can you take to foster open communication and mutual respect in your team?

_____

_____

_____

_____

_____

_____

Actionable Steps:

1. Schedule regular interdisciplinary huddles to discuss updates, share insights, and address challenges collaboratively.

2. Use standardized communication tools like SBARQ to ensure clarity and alignment across teams.

3. Identify a collaborative initiative, such as a quality improvement project, and involve representatives from multiple disciplines to drive innovation and teamwork.

Notes:

_____

_____

_____

_____

_____

_____

_____

_____

_____

_____

_____

_____

14

BREAKING THROUGH THE NOISE: COMMUNICATION THAT INSPIRES

The Heart of Leadership Communication

Effective communication is the backbone of leadership, yet it often feels like one of the most challenging aspects of the role. As a nurse leader, you are tasked with delivering messages that not only inform but also inspire, align, and motivate your team. With the noise of daily operations, constant demands, and varying team dynamics, how do you ensure your voice is heard? Clear, authentic communication that is tailored to your audience and rooted in empathy sets the foundation for trust and collaboration. This chapter explores how nurse leaders can craft impactful messages, adapt to diverse situations, and overcome communication barriers while inspiring action and engagement.

Crafting Messages That Connect

Leadership communication is not just about what you

say but how you say it. Messages that resonate with your team are those that are clear, concise, and tailored to their needs. Start by considering the purpose of your communication. Are you sharing information, addressing concerns, or motivating your team? Each purpose demands a unique approach to ensure the message is impactful.

For example, when announcing a change in workflow, it's essential to highlight not only the what and how but also the why. Team members are more likely to embrace change when they understand its purpose and potential benefits. Rather than framing the change as an order, position it as a solution to a shared challenge. A leader who communicates with empathy and clarity fosters an environment of openness and trust, making transitions smoother for the team.

Additionally, tone and delivery play a significant role in crafting messages that connect. Messages delivered with confidence and warmth are more likely to resonate than those perceived as rushed or impersonal. Leaders should also consider the medium of communication, whether it's a formal email, a casual huddle, or an individual conversation, and adapt accordingly.

Adapting Your Communication Style

Different situations and audiences require different communication styles. A one-size-fits-all approach often leads to misunderstandings or missed opportunities. Leaders must be flexible, tailoring their delivery to fit the context and audience while maintaining consistency in their overall messaging.

- One-on-One Conversations: These settings are ideal for addressing sensitive topics, providing feedback, or understanding individual concerns. Use active listening techniques, such as reflecting back key points, to show that you are fully engaged. Asking open-ended questions encourages the other person to share their thoughts, fostering a deeper connection.

- Team Meetings: These larger group settings require clear, concise messaging to keep everyone aligned. Avoid overwhelming your audience with excessive details; instead, use bullet points, visual aids, or handouts to reinforce your message. Encourage team members to ask questions or provide feedback, creating a collaborative atmosphere.

- Interdisciplinary Communication: Collaborating across departments requires emphasizing shared goals, such as improving patient outcomes. Focus on framing messages in a way that highlights mutual benefits, and remain open to different perspectives to build bridges across specialties.

Inspiring Through Storytelling

Stories have the unique power to engage emotions, foster connections, and inspire action. As a leader, sharing stories about your own experiences or those of your team can create a sense of shared purpose and motivation. Unlike data-driven presentations or procedural updates, stories humanize your message and make it more memorable.

For instance, recounting how a nurse's quick thinking improved patient outcomes can reinforce the importance of teamwork and clinical judgment. Stories that highlight resilience or innovation during challenges serve as powerful reminders of your team's capability and value. When using storytelling, ensure the narrative aligns with the message you want to convey, whether it's about perseverance, growth, or collaboration.

Case Study: A leader shared a story during a huddle about a nurse who overcame initial struggles with a new technology system and later became the unit's go-to resource for troubleshooting. This story inspired the team to embrace challenges as opportunities for growth.

Balancing Transparency and Diplomacy

Leaders often walk a fine line between transparency and diplomacy. While honesty builds trust, sharing too much information (especially in high-stress situations) can overwhelm or demoralize your team. Conversely, withholding important details can breed mistrust. Knowing what to share, when, and how requires careful judgment and emotional intelligence.

For example, when addressing budget constraints, a leader might transparently outline the challenges while emphasizing steps being taken to address them. It's crucial to frame the conversation in a way that reassures the team of your commitment to advocating for their needs without sugarcoating the reality. Diplomatic transparency fosters trust while maintaining focus on solutions.

Overcoming Barriers to Effective Communication

Even the most skilled leaders encounter barriers to

effective communication. These challenges can range from time constraints to misinterpretation of messages and heightened emotions during high-stress situations. Addressing these obstacles requires intentional strategies to ensure clarity, connection, and understanding.

Time constraints are a common barrier in fast-paced environments like healthcare, where leaders must juggle competing priorities. Finding time for meaningful conversations can feel impossible, but even brief, intentional touchpoints can have a significant impact. For example, a quick two-minute check-in with a team member before a shift can clarify expectations and strengthen rapport. Leaders who prioritize these moments create an environment where communication remains a priority, despite the hectic pace of daily operations.

Misinterpretation is another frequent challenge, particularly with written communication like emails or memos. Messages conveyed through text can lack the tone and context needed for full understanding, leading to confusion or unintended offense. To mitigate this, leaders should follow up written messages with verbal clarification when possible, especially for complex or sensitive topics. Additionally, asking team members to summarize key takeaways ensures alignment and provides an opportunity to address misunderstandings.

Emotional reactions can also disrupt effective communication. In high-stress situations, heightened emotions may cloud judgment or cause individuals to react defensively. Leaders can navigate these moments by acknowledging emotions before moving toward solutions. For example, a leader addressing a team's frustration about staffing shortages might begin by saying, "I understand how overwhelming this feels, and I want to hear your thoughts before we discuss possible solutions." This approach validates team members' feelings while setting a constructive tone for the conversation.

By proactively addressing these barriers, leaders can enhance their communication skills and foster an environment of clarity and trust. Regularly reflecting on past communication challenges and seeking feedback from peers and team members can further improve a leader's ability to connect effectively.

Communicating with Purpose and Passion

Leadership communication is more than a skill... it's a responsibility. By crafting messages that connect, adapting your style, and balancing transparency with diplomacy, you ensure that your voice not only cuts through the noise but also inspires and unites your team. In the fast-paced world of nursing, your ability to communicate effectively is a powerful tool for driving positive change and fostering a cohesive team culture.

Reflection Prompts:

How do you currently adapt your communication style to different situations? Where could you improve?

_____

_____

_____

_____

_____

_____

Think about a time when storytelling could have enhanced your message. How can you incorporate storytelling into future communications?

_____

_____

_____

_____

_____

_____

What steps can you take to balance transparency and diplomacy in challenging conversations?

_____

_____

_____

_____

_____

_____

Actionable Steps:

1. Create a "story bank" of impactful moments to use in future team meetings or motivational speeches.

2. Schedule regular one-on-one check-ins with team members to ensure open and clear communication.

3. Practice adapting your communication style by role-playing scenarios with a trusted colleague or mentor.

Notes:

_____

_____

_____

_____

_____

_____

_____

_____

_____

_____

_____

_____

_____

15

EMPHASIZING CAREER GROWTH IN YOUR TEAM

The Leader's Role in Career Development

Great leaders don't just focus on day-to-day operations, they invest in their team's growth. By encouraging career development, leaders inspire motivation, foster loyalty, and help individuals realize their full potential. As a nurse leader, your role is to create an environment where team members feel supported in pursuing their goals, whether that means advancing within their current roles, obtaining certifications, or taking on leadership positions themselves. Career growth can be more than a benefit for individual. It can be a powerful tool for strengthening the entire team.

Understanding Team Members' Goals

Career growth has to begin with understanding the aspirations of your team members. Each nurse brings unique goals to their role, shaped by their personal interests, professional experiences, and long-term plans. Some may aim to specialize in a particular clinical area, while others may aspire to leadership positions or advanced degrees. As a leader, your first step is to uncover these goals through open and honest communication.

During one-on-one meetings or rounding, take the time to ask thoughtful questions that encourage team members to share their ambitions. Questions like, "What professional goals are you working toward?" or "Where do you see yourself in five years?" not only demonstrate your interest in their success but also give you the insight needed to align opportunities with their objectives. For instance, if a nurse expresses interest in leadership, you might recommend they take on a charge nurse role to gain experience managing a team. Alternatively, a nurse passionate about research could be introduced to ongoing clinical trials or quality improvement initiatives within the organization.

Beyond identifying goals, it's equally important to revisit these conversations regularly. As team members grow and evolve, their aspirations may change. Continuous dialogue ensures you remain aligned with their current needs and can provide timely support.

Case Study: During a performance review, a nurse revealed a long-standing interest in quality improvement but lacked the confidence to take on such a role. Recognizing their potential, the leader connected them with a hospital committee focused on patient outcomes, providing mentorship and resources to help them succeed. This not only advanced the nurse's career but also brought fresh insights back to the unit from the committee's work.

Providing Growth Opportunities

Opportunities for growth don't occur by chance. They require intentional effort and thoughtful planning. As a leader, it's your responsibility to identify ways to challenge your team while ensuring they have the resources and support to succeed. Growth opportunities can take many forms, from formal education to on-the-job experiences, each tailored to the needs of the individual and the team.

Educational support is one of the most accessible ways to foster career development. Encouraging team members to attend workshops, conferences, or online courses expands their knowledge and keeps them engaged in their work. Many organizations offer tuition reimbursement or funding for professional development; as a leader, advocate for these resources and ensure your team is aware of them.

Another impactful strategy is promoting certifications and specializations. For example, a perioperative nurse might benefit from obtaining CNOR certification, while a pediatric nurse could pursue CPN certification. Certifications not only enhance the nurse's expertise but also elevate the team's overall quality of care. Leaders can support this process by providing study resources, flexible scheduling, or financial assistance.

On-the-job experiences, such as informal leadership roles, are equally valuable. Assigning team members to act as charge nurse, preceptor, or project lead allows them to develop leadership skills and gain confidence in their abilities. These roles also provide insight into team dynamics, preparing them for more advanced positions in the future.

Mentorship as a Growth Tool

Mentorship is a cornerstone of professional development, offering a structured yet personal approach to growth. By pairing less experienced nurses with seasoned mentors, leaders can create relationships where guidance, learning, and encouragement flow naturally. A strong mentorship program fosters a culture of collaboration and ensures that knowledge is passed down effectively within the team.

As a leader, your role in facilitating mentorship begins with identifying potential pairings. Look for mentors whose skills and experiences align with the mentee's goals. For example, a nurse pursuing advanced practice might benefit from mentorship with a nurse practitioner, while someone interested in leadership could learn from an experienced charge nurse or manager. Beyond creating these pairings, leaders should establish clear guidelines for mentorship, such as setting regular meeting times and defining measurable objectives.

Leading by example is another powerful way to emphasize mentorship's value. By serving as a mentor yourself, you demonstrate your commitment to the team's growth and provide a direct link between leadership and professional development.

Actionable Tool: Develop a mentorship program within your department. Include specific guidelines, such as setting goals for the mentorship period, and schedule regular feedback sessions to assess its success.

Celebrating Growth and Achievements

Acknowledging and celebrating milestones is an often-overlooked but vital aspect of fostering career growth. Recognition not only reinforces the value of hard work but also motivates team members to continue pursuing their goals. Celebrations can range from informal acknowledgments to formal events, depending on the significance of the achievement.

For instance, highlighting accomplishments during team meetings or sending a congratulatory email shows team members that their efforts are noticed. Hosting a recognition event for team members who have earned certifications, completed training programs, or taken on new roles creates a sense of pride and community. By tying these celebrations to the broader goals of the team, leaders can emphasize how individual achievements contribute to collective success.

Overcoming Barriers to Career Growth

Despite the many benefits of career development, barriers often arise that can hinder progress. These challenges may include limited resources, heavy workloads, or a lack of confidence among team members. Leaders must proactively address these obstacles to ensure growth remains a priority.

One common barrier is financial constraints, which can discourage team members from pursuing certifications or advanced education. As a leader, explore funding options within the organization or through local professional associations. Advocating for tuition reimbursement programs or department-sponsored certifications can significantly reduce financial burdens.

Workload demands are another frequent challenge.

Nurses may hesitate to take on new responsibilities or enroll in training programs due to concerns about balancing these commitments with their existing workload. Leaders can help by reallocating duties, providing flexible scheduling, or offering additional support during transitional periods.

A lack of confidence can prevent team members from pursuing their goals. Encouraging them to take small, manageable steps such as shadowing a mentor or participating in a short-term project can build their self-assurance and set them on the path to success.

Growth as a Shared Success

Fostering career growth within your team is one of the most rewarding aspects of leadership. By understanding individual goals, providing meaningful opportunities, facilitating mentorship, and celebrating achievements, you create a culture of growth and engagement. Investing in your team's success doesn't just strengthen individuals; it builds a more capable, motivated, and cohesive team ready to tackle challenges together.

Reflection Prompts:

How well do you understand the career goals of your team members? What steps can you take to learn more?

_____

_____

_____

_____

_____

_____

What opportunities for growth currently exist within your organization, and how can you connect your team to them?

_____

_____

_____

_____

_____

_____

How can you ensure that career development remains a priority despite competing demands?

_____

_____

_____

_____

_____

_____

Actionable Steps:

1. Schedule one-on-one meetings with team members to discuss their professional goals and identify areas where you can provide support.

2. Research available resources within your organization for career development, such as funding for certifications or professional memberships.

3. Create a recognition plan to celebrate team achievements, ensuring milestones are acknowledged regularly.

Notes:

_____

_____

_____

_____

_____

_____

_____

_____

_____

_____

_____

_____

Part IV: Leading in the Bigger Picture

16

LEADING THROUGH CHANGE

The Leader as a Guide Through Transition

Change is inevitable in healthcare, whether it comes in the form of new technologies, updated policies, or shifts in team dynamics. As a nurse leader, your role during these transitions is pivotal. You are not only responsible for implementing change but also for guiding your team through the uncertainty and resistance that often accompanies it. Effective change leadership requires empathy, communication, and strategic planning. This chapter explores the complexities of leading through change and offers actionable strategies for fostering adaptability and maintaining morale during transitions.

Understanding Resistance to Change

Resistance to change is a natural human response. In healthcare, where routines and systems are critical to patient safety, even small changes can feel disruptive. Team members may fear the unknown, worry about their ability to adapt, or question the necessity of the change. As a leader, it's essential to approach resistance with empathy and curiosity rather than frustration.

Start by acknowledging your team's concerns. For instance, if new charting software is being introduced, recognize the extra time and effort required for staff to learn the system. Addressing these concerns openly demonstrates that you understand their challenges and value their perspectives.

Listening is equally important. Provide opportunities for team members to voice their concerns, either in team meetings or one-on-one conversations. By understanding the root of their resistance, whether it's fear of failure, lack of information, or dissatisfaction with past changes, you can tailor your approach to address their specific needs.

Expanded Insight: Think about a time when your team resisted a change. How did you approach their concerns, and what did you learn from the experience? How might you handle a similar situation differently in the future?

Communicating the Why Behind the Change

One of the most effective ways to ease resistance and build engagement is by clearly communicating the purpose of the change. People are more likely to embrace change when they understand its rationale, see its potential benefits, and feel connected to the larger mission behind it. As a leader, your role is to bridge the gap between organizational goals and team buy-in by providing transparent, consistent, and meaningful communication.

Start by outlining the "why" behind the change. Whether the goal is to improve patient outcomes, streamline workflows, or address safety concerns, explaining the broader impact helps team members see beyond immediate inconveniences. For instance, when introducing a new patient documentation system, you might emphasize how it reduces redundancies, saves time, and ensures more accurate record-keeping, ultimately benefiting both staff and patients. Using concrete data, case studies, or examples from other successful implementations can further strengthen the message.

However, communication shouldn't end with the initial explanation. Ongoing updates are critical to maintaining transparency and building trust throughout the process. A highly effective tool for this is the stoplight report: a simple, visual system that tracks progress using green, yellow, and red indicators. Green signifies completed tasks, yellow represents work in progress, and red highlights areas facing challenges or delays.

The stoplight report can be displayed in a central area of the unit, such as a break room or main workstation, where staff frequently gather. By updating it regularly, leaders ensure that the team stays informed about progress without requiring constant formal updates. This passive communication method not only reinforces transparency but also fosters a sense of shared accountability and momentum.

For example, during the rollout of a new scheduling platform, a nurse manager implemented a stoplight report to track three key phases: staff training, system testing, and go-live readiness. Each phase was broken down into smaller tasks, with their status clearly indicated on the report. Staff could see at a glance what had been accomplished, what was underway, and where additional support was needed. This approach reduced confusion, built excitement as progress was visibly marked, and encouraged team members to contribute to resolving red-light challenges.

In addition to tools like the stoplight report, regular meetings or updates through emails and team huddles can provide further clarity and address emerging questions. Encouraging feedback and actively listening to staff concerns during these updates creates a two-way communication channel, strengthening trust and collaboration.

Expanded Insight: Think about your current approach to communicating change. How could tools like a stoplight report or regular updates improve clarity and engagement with your team?

Engaging Your Team in the Change Process

Involving your team in the change process can significantly increase buy-in and reduce resistance. When staff feel that their voices are heard and their contributions matter, they are more likely to support the change.

Engagement can take many forms. For instance, you might create a task force of team members to pilot the change, gather feedback, and suggest improvements. Alternatively, host brainstorming sessions to identify potential challenges and collaboratively develop solutions.

Empowering staff to take ownership of the change

not only enhances their commitment but also leverages their expertise to ensure a smoother implementation. For example, a nurse leader introducing a new medication administration protocol might involve senior nurses in developing training materials, ensuring that they are both practical and relevant to the team's needs.

Providing Support During Transition

Change can be stressful, particularly in high-pressure environments like healthcare. As a leader, your role is to provide the resources, training, and emotional support your team needs to navigate the transition successfully.

Training is a critical component of support. Ensure that staff have access to comprehensive, hands-on training sessions where they can practice new skills in a low-stakes environment. Pairing less experienced staff with mentors or "change champions" can also provide additional guidance and reassurance.

Equally important is addressing the emotional impact of change. Regular check-ins allow you to gauge team morale and address concerns early. Simple gestures, such as expressing gratitude for their efforts or celebrating small milestones, can boost morale and remind your team that their hard work is appreciated.

Leading by Example During Change

Leadership during change requires more than issuing directives, it demands leading by example. Your attitude and actions set the tone for how the team approaches the transition. If you remain calm, optimistic, and solution-focused, your team is more likely to adopt the same mindset.

For instance, a leader who proactively learns a new process and demonstrates it during team meetings not only shows their commitment but also builds confidence among staff. By openly addressing your own challenges or uncertainties, you normalize the learning curve and reinforce the message that adapting to change is a team effort.

Celebrating Progress and Success

Acknowledging progress and celebrating successes, no matter how small, can help sustain momentum during challenging transitions. Recognition reinforces the value of the team's efforts and boosts morale.

Celebrations don't need to be elaborate. A simple "thank you" during a meeting, a handwritten note, or a small team lunch can go a long way in showing appreciation. Additionally, highlighting how the change has positively impacted patients or workflows can reinforce its benefits and build enthusiasm for future initiatives.

Navigating Change with Confidence

Leading through change is such a challenging aspect of leadership that there are entire books and theories dedicated to the subject. It is also one of the most rewarding experiences you will face. By understanding resistance, communicating effectively, engaging your team, and providing support, you can guide your team through transitions with confidence and compassion. Change is not just about implementing new processes, it's about fostering a culture of adaptability and resilience that empowers your team to thrive in an ever-evolving healthcare landscape.

Reflection Prompts:

Think of a recent change in your organization. How did you approach resistance, and what could you have done differently?

_____

_____

_____

_____

_____

_____

How do you currently communicate the purpose of changes to your team? What strategies could improve transparency and understanding?

_____

_____

_____

_____

_____

_____

What steps can you take to involve your team more actively in future changes?

_____

_____

_____

_____

_____

Actionable Steps:

1. Identify an upcoming change and create a communication plan that includes regular updates and opportunities for feedback.

2. Develop a support strategy, such as scheduling training sessions or assigning change champions, to ease the transition for your team.

3. Plan a recognition event or gesture to celebrate your team's progress during a current or recent change initiative.

Notes:

_____

_____

_____

_____

_____

_____

_____

_____

_____

_____

_____

_____

_____

_____

17

THE POWER OF OPENNESS: EMBRACING CHANGE AND FLEXIBILITY

Openness as a Leadership Strength

In the constantly changing landscape of healthcare, adaptability is an essential skill that cannot be overstated. Effective leaders embrace change and demonstrate openness to new ideas, perspectives, and possibilities. This mindset not only fosters innovation but also builds resilience within teams, enabling them to thrive in uncertain or challenging situations. Leading with openness and flexibility requires a willingness to listen, learn, and adjust, even when it means stepping outside of your comfort zone. In this chapter, we'll explore how adaptability strengthens leadership, strategies for cultivating openness, and the impact of flexibility on team morale and success.

Understanding the Value of Adaptability

Adaptability is the ability to adjust your approach in

response to new information or changing circumstances. It is a hallmark of strong leadership, as it demonstrates a commitment to problem-solving and continuous improvement. Leaders who resist change risk stagnation, while those who embrace it inspire growth and innovation.

For instance, consider a leader who must navigate a sudden staffing shortage. An adaptable leader quickly assesses the situation, reallocates resources, and communicates a clear plan to maintain patient care. Their flexibility not only ensures operational continuity but also instills confidence in the team.

Being adaptable also means recognizing that no single solution fits every problem. Leaders who remain open to experimenting with new approaches, whether by seeking input from their team, adopting emerging technologies, or revisiting established processes, create a culture of learning and collaboration.

Cultivating Openness in Leadership

Openness should be more than a willingness to consider new ideas; it's should be treated as a mindset that encourages transparency, active listening, and humility. Leaders who practice openness foster trust and psychological safety, creating an environment where team members feel valued and empowered to share their perspectives.

To cultivate openness, start by actively soliciting feedback. This might involve structured methods, such as anonymous surveys, or informal one-on-one conversations. When team members see that their input is taken seriously, they are more likely to contribute innovative ideas and solutions.

Another key aspect of openness is maintaining transparency about your decision-making process. For example, if you decide to implement a new policy based on staff feedback, explain how their input influenced the decision. This not only reinforces the importance of their contributions but also demonstrates your commitment to collaborative leadership.

Case Study: A nurse leader introduced a new patient handoff protocol after consulting staff about challenges with the existing process. By openly discussing the feedback and inviting staff to participate in the pilot phase, the leader ensured a smoother implementation and greater team buy-in.

Flexibility in Decision-Making

Flexibility in leadership doesn't always mean indecisiveness. It can just as much mean the willingness to adjust your plans when circumstances change. Leaders who cling rigidly to a single course of action risk alienating their teams and missing opportunities for improvement. Effective flexibility involves balancing a clear strategic vision with the readiness to pivot when needed.

For example, a leader might implement a new workflow only to discover unintended bottlenecks. Rather than doubling down on the original plan, they gather input from the team, reassess the process, and make necessary adjustments. This adaptability signals to the team that the leader prioritizes outcomes over ego, strengthening trust and collaboration.

Key principles of flexible decision-making include:

- Assessing the Situation Regularly: Revisit decisions periodically to ensure they're still effective. Situations in healthcare evolve quickly, and what works today might not work tomorrow.

- Involving the Team: Seek feedback from your team to identify potential adjustments. Their on-the-ground perspective often reveals solutions that may not be immediately apparent.

- Being Open to Change: Acknowledge when a plan isn't working as intended. Flexibility doesn't equate to failure; it shows a willingness to refine strategies for the best outcome.

- Communicating Changes Clearly: When adjustments are made, explain the reasons behind them and how they address team concerns or improve outcomes.

The Impact of Openness on Team Dynamics

Leading with openness and flexibility has a profound impact on team dynamics. When leaders model these qualities, they set the tone for a culture of mutual respect and adaptability. Teams that operate in an open environment are more likely to embrace change, collaborate effectively, and innovate solutions to challenges.

For instance, when a team feels empowered to share ideas without fear of judgment, they contribute more actively to problem-solving and decision-making. Similarly, a flexible leader who adjusts workloads to accommodate individual needs demonstrates that they value their team members as people, not just as contributors to outcomes. This builds loyalty and morale, ensuring long-term engagement and productivity.

Thriving Through Openness and Flexibility

Leadership in healthcare demands the ability to navigate constant change with grace and resilience. By cultivating openness and flexibility, leaders create environments where teams feel supported, valued, and empowered to succeed. Adaptability not only ensures operational success but also fosters a culture of trust and collaboration, preparing teams to face future challenges with confidence and creativity.

Reflection Prompts:

Think of a recent situation where adaptability or flexibility led to a positive outcome. What did you learn from that experience?

_____

_____

_____

_____

_____

_____

How can you create more opportunities for your team to share feedback and contribute to decision-making processes?

_____

_____

_____

_____

_____

_____

In what ways could you demonstrate greater openness to new ideas or perspectives in your leadership role?

_____

_____

_____

_____

_____

Actionable Steps:

1. Schedule regular feedback sessions with your team to discuss challenges, opportunities, and potential improvements.

2. Identify one area of your leadership approach where you could show greater flexibility and commit to making adjustments this month.

3. Model adaptability by sharing an example of a time when you adjusted your plans based on team input or changing circumstances.

Notes:

18

ADVOCATING FOR NURSES AND THE PROFESSION

The Nurse Leader as an Advocate

Advocacy is a cornerstone of nursing leadership. As a nurse leader, your role extends beyond managing teams and improving workflows; you are also a vital voice for your staff and the nursing profession as a whole. Whether you're addressing workplace challenges, influencing policy, or championing professional development, advocacy requires courage, strategic thinking, and an unwavering commitment to the well-being of nurses and the patients they serve. This chapter explores the multi-faceted role of advocacy in nursing leadership, offering insights and strategies to empower leaders to effect meaningful change.

Understanding the Scope of Advocacy

Advocacy in nursing leadership operates on multiple levels: individual, organizational, and professional. Each level presents unique challenges and opportunities to make a difference.

At the individual level, advocacy involves supporting team members in their personal and professional growth. For example, a nurse leader advocating for flexible scheduling to accommodate a staff member pursuing further education demonstrates advocacy on a personal scale. Organizational advocacy, meanwhile, focuses on improving workplace conditions, securing resources, and addressing systemic issues. A leader lobbying for additional staffing to reduce workloads or advocating for updated equipment to enhance patient safety reflects organizational-level advocacy. Professional advocacy involves championing the nursing profession on a broader scale, such as participating in policy development, contributing to professional associations, or raising awareness of nursing's critical role in healthcare. Leaders who use their platform to influence legislation or promote the value of nursing in interdisciplinary teams embody this type of advocacy.

Each level is interconnected, and effective advocacy often involves navigating between them to address immediate needs while advancing long-term goals. Leaders who understand these layers can tailor their advocacy efforts to achieve meaningful impacts on their teams and the profession as a whole.

Case Study: A nurse leader noticed high turnover among new graduate nurses due to a lack of structured mentorship. They advocated for the creation of a formal mentorship program, pairing experienced nurses with new hires to foster connection, reduce burnout, and improve retention.

Advocating for Staff Well-Being

Staff well-being is a fundamental component of leadership advocacy. Nurses frequently face high stress, long hours, and emotional demands, all of which can contribute to burnout. As a leader, advocating for your team's mental and physical health is critical to fostering a supportive and sustainable work environment.

Creating a culture of self-care within your team is an essential starting point. Encouraging practices such as mindfulness, peer support programs, and designated wellness spaces helps staff decompress and recharge. Additionally, addressing burnout proactively by monitoring staffing ratios and advocating for manageable workloads demonstrates your commitment to their well-being. Open communication is equally important. Establishing regular check-ins where team members feel safe sharing their challenges and stressors allows leaders to address concerns early and offer support.

For example, a nurse leader who works with hospital administration to implement a rotating "wellness day" policy, allowing nurses a paid day off for self-care, demonstrates meaningful advocacy. Such actions improve staff satisfaction and contribute to a healthier work environment. By prioritizing staff well-being, leaders strengthen their teams and create a foundation for long-term success.

Engaging in Organizational Advocacy

Nurse leaders have a unique vantage point, bridging the gap between frontline staff and organizational decision-makers. This position enables them to advocate for systemic improvements that benefit both nurses and patients. Building strong relationships with executives and administrators is crucial for gaining support for initiatives. Presenting evidence-based proposals that highlight the benefits of addressing issues like staffing shortages or resource allocation can effectively build your case.

Using data is another powerful tool in organizational advocacy. Metrics such as patient outcomes, staff turnover rates, and satisfaction surveys provide compelling arguments for change. For example, demonstrating how understaffing correlates with increased patient safety incidents can strengthen your efforts to secure additional resources. Empowering staff to share their insights and participate in committees further amplifies advocacy efforts. This collaborative approach not only drives meaningful progress but also fosters a sense of shared ownership and accountability.

Becoming a Voice for the Profession

Advocating for the nursing profession requires engaging with broader issues that affect healthcare policy and practice. Nurse leaders are uniquely positioned to shape the future of nursing by raising awareness of the profession's contributions and challenges. Participating in policy development through organizations like the American Nurses Association (ANA) allows leaders to influence legislation and promote the interests of nurses nationwide. Public awareness campaigns highlighting the critical role of nurses during public health crises elevate the profession's visibility and recognition.

Mentorship and education are also integral to professional advocacy. Supporting scholarships, participating in academic partnerships, or mentoring students ensures that future generations of nurses are prepared to excel. For example, a nurse leader who participates in a state-level task force addressing the nursing shortage contributes to initiatives like tuition reimbursement programs, which increase enrollment in nursing programs and strengthen the workforce.

Actionable Tool: Join an interdisciplinary committee within your workplace to gain access to elevated advocacy opportunities and resources. Commit to attending at least one policy-related event or meeting a quarter.

Overcoming Barriers to Advocacy

Advocacy is not without its challenges. Leaders often face resistance from administrators, budget constraints, or skepticism from peers. Navigating these barriers requires persistence, creativity, and strategic planning. Building consensus is key when encountering pushback. Framing advocacy efforts as solutions that benefit multiple stakeholders, such as improving patient outcomes while enhancing staff satisfaction, increases the likelihood of support.

Balancing advocacy with operational demands can also be challenging. Advocacy efforts often compete with the day-to-day responsibilities of leadership. Prioritizing initiatives that align with organizational goals ensures support and sustainability. Staying informed about industry trends, policy developments, and emerging best practices further strengthens advocacy efforts, enabling leaders to approach challenges with confidence and clarity.

Advocacy as a Leadership Imperative

Advocacy should be treated as an opportunity to shape the future of nursing and healthcare. By championing the needs of your team, addressing systemic challenges, and elevating the profession, you empower nurses to thrive and ensure patients receive the highest quality of care. Advocacy is not always easy, but it is one of the most impactful ways leaders can make a lasting difference. Nurse leaders who embrace their role as advocates inspire positive change and leave a meaningful legacy in their organizations and communities.

Reflection Prompts:

What is one area where your team needs advocacy, and how can you begin addressing it?

_____

_____

_____

_____

_____

_____

How can you balance advocating for your staff's needs with fulfilling organizational responsibilities?

_____

_____

_____

_____

_____

_____

In what ways can you contribute to advancing the nursing profession beyond your immediate workplace?

_____

_____

_____

_____

_____

Actionable Steps:

1. Identify a pressing challenge within your team or organization and develop an advocacy plan to address it, including key stakeholders and potential solutions.

2. Join a professional organization or committee to participate in advocacy efforts beyond your unit.

3. Schedule a meeting with hospital leadership to discuss a staff-centered initiative, presenting data and actionable recommendations.

Notes:

_____

_____

_____

_____

_____

_____

_____

_____

_____

_____

_____

19

QUALITY IMPROVEMENT AND PATIENT SAFETY: A LEADER'S ROLE

The Nurse Leader's Commitment to Quality and Safety

Quality improvement (QI) and patient safety are the cornerstones of effective healthcare delivery. For nurse leaders, these responsibilities extend beyond compliance with protocols; they require proactive initiatives, innovative thinking, and a relentless focus on outcomes. This chapter explores how nurse leaders can effectively drive QI efforts and create a culture of safety within their teams and organizations. It offers practical strategies, tools, and insights to help leaders navigate this critical aspect of their role.

Understanding Quality Improvement in Nursing

Quality improvement refers to the systematic efforts to enhance patient care by refining processes, reducing errors, and increasing efficiency. In nursing, QI projects are rooted in evidence-based practices and require collaboration across disciplines.

For example, a QI initiative to reduce hospital-acquired infections (HAIs) might involve auditing hand hygiene practices, implementing standardized protocols, and providing ongoing education to staff. These efforts not only improve patient outcomes but also boost team morale by demonstrating the tangible impact of their work.

As a leader, it's essential to view QI as a continuous cycle rather than a one-time effort. The *Plan-Do-Study-Act (PDSA)* model is a widely used framework for QI projects, guiding teams through iterative improvements. Nurse leaders play a pivotal role in facilitating this process, ensuring that goals are clear, data is collected accurately, and adjustments are made as needed.

The Role of Data in Quality Improvement

Data is the foundation of any successful QI initiative. By analyzing metrics such as patient outcomes, staff performance, and workflow efficiency, nurse leaders can identify areas for improvement and measure the success of interventions.

To make data actionable, leaders should focus on clarity and accessibility. Visual tools like dashboards or scorecards can help teams understand key performance indicators (KPIs) and track progress. For example, a dashboard displaying rates of patient falls by unit can motivate staff to engage in prevention efforts.

Leaders should also encourage a culture of transparency when it comes to data. Sharing successes and challenges openly with the team fosters trust and promotes collective ownership of quality goals.

Expanded Insight: How effectively does your current team use data to inform decision-making? What steps can you take to improve the visibility and accessibility of key metrics?

Fostering a Culture of Safety

Patient safety is inseparable from quality improvement. Leaders must create an environment where safety is prioritized, and staff feel empowered to speak up about risks or concerns.

One way to foster a culture of safety is through just culture principles, which emphasize learning and accountability rather than punishment. When errors occur, leaders should focus on understanding the root causes and implementing system-level changes rather than assigning blame. For example, if a medication error occurs, analyzing factors like workload, communication gaps, or system design can lead to meaningful improvements.

Leaders should also model safety behaviors, such as adhering to infection control protocols and encouraging open dialogue during safety huddles. These actions demonstrate a commitment to safety and reinforce its importance to the team.

Leading Quality Improvement Projects

Nurse leaders are often at the forefront of QI initiatives, responsible for assembling teams, setting goals, and driving implementation. Successful projects require a structured approach and strong collaboration.

Start by defining a clear objective. For example, if the goal is to reduce readmission rates, specify a target percentage and timeframe. Assemble a multidisciplinary team that includes nurses, physicians, administrators, and other stakeholders who can contribute diverse perspectives.

Engage staff by connecting the project's goals to their day-to-day work. For instance, explain how reducing readmissions improves not only patient outcomes but also staff workloads and morale. Regular updates and celebrations of progress keep teams motivated and invested in the project.

Case Study: A nurse leader led a QI project to improve discharge planning for heart failure patients. By implementing a standardized checklist, coordinating with case managers, and providing follow-up phone calls, the team reduced readmission rates by 15% within six months.

Overcoming Barriers to Quality Improvement

Despite its importance, QI efforts often face challenges such as limited resources, resistance to change, and competing priorities. Nurse leaders must navigate these obstacles with creativity and persistence.

To address resource constraints, leaders can advocate for funding or explore alternative solutions, such as reallocating existing resources or partnering with community organizations. Overcoming resistance requires engaging staff early in the process and highlighting the benefits of change. For example, framing a new workflow as a way to reduce stress or improve patient satisfaction can increase buy-in.

Leaders should also balance QI efforts with other responsibilities by integrating initiatives into existing workflows. For example, incorporating QI discussions into regular staff meetings ensures that improvement efforts remain a priority without adding extra meetings to the schedule.

The Ongoing Journey of Quality and Safety

Much like leadership as a whole, quality improvement and patient safety are not destinations but ongoing journeys that require dedication, collaboration, and innovation. As nurse leaders, your role in these efforts is pivotal, shaping the culture, processes, and outcomes of your team and organization. By leveraging data, fostering safety, and leading with purpose, you can drive meaningful change and set a standard of excellence in patient care.

Reflection Prompts:

What are the current quality and safety challenges in your unit, and how can you begin addressing them?

_____

_____

_____

_____

_____

_____

How does your team use data to identify areas for improvement and track progress?

_____

_____

_____

_____

_____

_____

What steps can you take to foster a culture where safety and quality are seen as shared responsibilities?

_____

_____

_____

_____

_____

Actionable Steps:

1. Implement the *PDSA cycle* for a small-scale QI project, involving your team in every step of the process.

2. Create a safety huddle checklist to encourage open communication and address potential risks proactively.

3. Create Develop a data dashboard to track key metrics and share updates with your team regularly.

Notes:

_____

_____

_____

_____

_____

_____

_____

_____

_____

_____

_____

_____

_____

20

MASTERING FINANCIAL MANAGEMENT: A KEY TO LEADERSHIP SUCCESS

The Importance of Financial Acumen in Nursing Leadership

Financial management is an essential yet often overlooked skill for nurse leaders. While many nurses transition into leadership roles with a strong clinical foundation, the financial responsibilities of managing budgets, allocating resources, and balancing cost-efficiency with quality care can feel daunting. This chapter demystifies financial management, providing practical strategies and insights to help nurse leaders confidently navigate this critical aspect of their role.

Understanding the Basics of Healthcare Finance

Healthcare finance operates at the intersection of patient care and organizational sustainability. Nurse leaders play a key role in managing unit budgets, monitoring expenses, and contributing to financial decisions that impact both staff and patients. Understanding basic financial concepts is the first step toward effective management.

Key terms to know include:

- Budgeting: The process of creating a financial plan for your unit, including projected income and expenses.
- Cost-Benefit Analysis: Evaluating the financial and non-financial outcomes of an initiative to determine its overall value.
- Revenue Cycle: The flow of funds into the organization, from patient billing to insurance reimbursements.

By familiarizing yourself with these concepts, you can better understand how financial decisions affect your unit and contribute to the organization's goals.

Expanded Insight: How comfortable are you with financial terminology and processes? What areas of healthcare finance would you like to learn more about?

Creating and Managing Budgets

Budgeting is one of the most tangible financial responsibilities for nurse leaders. A well-managed budget ensures that your unit has the resources it needs while aligning with organizational priorities.

To create a budget, start by reviewing historical data, such as staffing costs, supply usage, and revenue trends. Identify areas where expenses can be optimized without compromising care quality. For example, implementing a centralized inventory system might reduce waste and save costs.

Regularly monitoring your budget is equally important. Monthly reviews of spending patterns allow you to identify variances and adjust plans as needed. Engaging your team in this process can also be beneficial. Staff input provides valuable insights into resource allocation and potential savings.

Balancing Cost and Quality

One headache often shared across newer leaders in healthcare operations is balancing cost-efficiency with quality care. Leaders must make difficult decisions, such as prioritizing certain initiatives over others or finding ways to do more with less.

The key to balancing cost and quality is data-driven decision-making. Metrics such as patient outcomes, satisfaction scores, and workflow efficiency provide insights into where resources are most effectively utilized. For example, investing in staff education might initially increase costs but lead to long-term savings by reducing errors and improving retention.

Communicating the rationale behind financial decisions is also critical. When staff understand how budget constraints align with organizational goals, they are more likely to support changes and contribute to cost-saving efforts.

Advocating for Resources

As a nurse leader, you may often find yourself advocating for additional resources, whether it's funding for new equipment, approval for more staffing, or support for professional development programs. Successful advocacy requires preparation, persistence, and the ability to align your request with organizational priorities.

Begin by gathering evidence to support your case. Data, such as increased patient volumes or staff turnover rates, strengthens your argument. Frame your request in terms of its impact on patient care, safety, and overall efficiency. For example, requesting new monitoring equipment can be tied to improved patient outcomes and reduced length of stay.

Building relationships with administrators and finance teams also increases your credibility. By demonstrating a solid understanding of financial constraints and offering solutions that benefit both the unit and the organization, you position yourself as a trusted advocate.

Overcoming Financial Challenges

Financial management is not without its challenges. Budget cuts, limited resources, and competing priorities often place nurse leaders in difficult positions. Navigating these challenges requires creativity, adaptability, and resilience.

One strategy is to focus on small, incremental changes that collectively make a significant impact. For instance, reducing energy consumption or optimizing supply orders can yield noticeable savings over time. Leaders should also explore external funding opportunities, such as grants or partnerships, to supplement budgets.

Another challenge is fostering a culture of financial awareness among staff. Educating your team about budget constraints and involving them in cost-saving initiatives encourages accountability and collaboration.

Expanded Insight: What financial challenges does your unit currently face? How can you engage your team in finding solutions?

Financial Leadership as a Strategic Advantage

Mastering financial management empowers nurse leaders to make informed decisions, advocate effectively for resources, and contribute to the sustainability of their organizations. By developing financial literacy, creating strategic budgets, and balancing cost with quality, you not only strengthen your leadership capabilities but also ensure that your unit thrives in a competitive and resource-conscious healthcare environment.

Reflection Prompts:

What steps can you take to improve your financial literacy and confidence?

_____

_____

_____

_____

_____

_____

How can you involve your team in managing budgets and identifying cost-saving opportunities?

_____

_____

_____

_____

_____

_____

What strategies can you use to advocate for resources in your organization?

_____

_____

_____

_____

_____

_____

Actionable Steps:

1. Partner with your organization's finance team to schedule a workshop on healthcare budgeting and financial management.

2. Create a cost-saving initiative in your unit, such as optimizing supply usage or reducing energy consumption, and track its impact over six months.

3. Develop a budget monitoring tool, such as a simple spreadsheet, to track monthly expenses and identify variances in real time.

Notes:

_____

_____

_____

_____

_____

_____

_____

_____

_____

_____

_____

21

CLINICAL KNOWLEDGE AS A CORNERSTONE OF LEADERSHIP

The Role of Clinical Expertise in Leadership

Leadership inside and outside of a healthcare setting is about maintaining credibility, earning trust, and leading by example. At the core of this is clinical expertise. A deep understanding of the clinical environment allows nurse leaders to make informed decisions, advocate effectively for their teams, and build strong relationships with staff and patients alike. This chapter explores how clinical knowledge serves as a foundation for leadership, the importance of ongoing education, and the value of rolling up your sleeves to work alongside your team when needed.

Why Clinical Knowledge Matters in Leadership

Clinical expertise is the backbone of effective nursing leadership. Leaders who maintain a connection to patient care gain a unique perspective on the challenges and opportunities within their teams. They can identify workflow inefficiencies, understand the nuances of patient needs, and advocate more effectively for resources and support.

For instance, a nurse leader with firsthand experience in perioperative care can better assess the impact of staffing shortages or outdated equipment on surgical outcomes. Their clinical insight allows them to present evidence-based solutions to administrators, ensuring that decisions are both practical and impactful.

Clinical knowledge also fosters trust and respect among team members. Nurses are more likely to follow a leader who understands the realities of their work and can provide guidance rooted in experience. This trust creates a stronger team dynamic, where staff feel supported and empowered to excel.

The Balance Between Leadership and Clinical Practice

One challenge nurse leaders often face is striking the right balance between administrative duties and maintaining clinical involvement. While leadership roles demand significant time and focus on operations, remaining connected to patient care is essential for credibility and decision-making.

Leaders can achieve this balance by periodically participating in clinical work, such as shadowing team members, assisting during peak times, or stepping in to cover shifts when needed. These actions not only reinforce their clinical skills but also demonstrate solidarity with their team.

Case Study: During a particularly busy flu season, a nurse leader in a pediatric hospital stepped onto the floor to assist with triage and patient care. Their willingness to work alongside staff alleviated some of the workload and boosted team morale. By showing they were willing to "roll up their sleeves," the leader strengthened trust and cohesion within the team.

Staying Current: Lifelong Learning in Leadership

The healthcare field is constantly evolving, with new technologies, treatments, and best practices emerging regularly. For nurse leaders, staying current with these advancements is not just beneficial, it's necessary. Leaders who prioritize ongoing education model a commitment to excellence and inspire their teams to do the same.

Attending conferences, pursuing certifications, and engaging in professional development opportunities are effective ways to stay informed. For example, a nurse leader specializing in critical care might obtain the CCRN certification to deepen their expertise. Additionally, participating in interdisciplinary rounds or quality improvement initiatives keeps leaders connected to the latest clinical advancements and reinforces their credibility.

Leaders should also encourage their teams to pursue continuing education. By advocating for funding, flexible scheduling, or institutional support for training programs, they create an environment where growth and learning are valued.

Leading by Example: The Value of Hands-On Leadership

Sometimes, the most powerful way to lead is by example. Nurse leaders who step into clinical roles when needed send a clear message: they are not above the challenges their team faces and are willing to share the workload. This approach not only builds trust but also allows leaders to experience the day-to-day realities of their team, leading to more informed and empathetic decision-making.

For example, a leader who assists in implementing a new electronic medical record system by participating in training sessions alongside their staff gains firsthand knowledge of the system's challenges and benefits. This insight allows them to address issues proactively and provide meaningful support during the transition.

Leading by example also creates opportunities to mentor and inspire staff. By demonstrating clinical excellence, leaders reinforce the importance of high standards and continuous improvement.

Building a Culture of Clinical Excellence

Nurse leaders play a pivotal role in fostering a culture of clinical excellence within their teams. This involves setting clear expectations for quality care, supporting professional growth, and celebrating achievements.

One effective strategy is to implement regular skills assessments or simulations to ensure staff maintain competency in critical areas. Leaders can also organize workshops, guest lectures, or journal clubs to encourage knowledge sharing and collaboration.

Recognizing and celebrating clinical achievements further reinforces this culture. Highlighting a nurse who implemented a successful patient safety initiative or earned a new certification shows the team that their expertise and efforts are valued.

Expanded Insight: Think about the current culture within your team. What practices already support clinical excellence, and where do you see opportunities for improvement? How can you, as a leader, encourage continuous learning and collaboration to elevate the standard of care?

Overcoming Challenges in Clinical Leadership

Balancing clinical and administrative responsibilities can also be a significant challenge for clinician leaders. Effective leadership requires staying connected to patient care while managing the broader operational needs of a unit or organization. This balance can be difficult to achieve, but with intentional strategies, leaders can remain grounded in clinical realities while fulfilling their administrative roles.

One of the most common challenges is the perception of distance between leadership and the clinical environment. Staff may feel that leaders are removed from the day-to-day realities of patient care, which can erode trust and create resistance. Leaders can address this by demonstrating their understanding of clinical challenges through active engagement. For example, participating in clinical rounds, assisting during peak times, or shadowing staff periodically reinforces credibility and shows a willingness to share in the team's efforts. Transparency also plays a critical role; leaders should communicate how their administrative decisions align with improving clinical outcomes and supporting staff.

Maintaining clinical competence is another hurdle. Leaders often fear losing touch with bedside care, which can diminish their confidence and the trust of their team. Regularly participating in professional development opportunities such as workshops, simulations, or certifications keep skills sharp and demonstrates a commitment to lifelong learning. For instance, a nurse leader in a critical care unit might attend advanced training sessions or participate in quality improvement projects, ensuring they remain an informed resource for their team.

Addressing resistance to change is perhaps the most emotionally taxing challenge. Nurses may push back on new policies or initiatives if they perceive them as disconnected from their needs. To overcome this, leaders should foster collaboration by involving staff in the decision-making process and seeking their input during planning stages. By framing changes as collective improvements rather than mandates, leaders build ownership and reduce resistance.

Overcoming these challenges requires persistence, empathy, and a proactive approach. Leaders who remain visible, informed, and engaged strengthen trust within their teams and set the stage for collaborative success.

Clinical Knowledge as a Pillar of Leadership

Clinical expertise is a cornerstone of nursing leadership, providing the foundation for credibility, trust, and informed decision-making. By staying connected to patient care, prioritizing ongoing education, and leading by example, nurse leaders not only enhance their effectiveness but also inspire their teams to achieve excellence. In a constantly evolving healthcare landscape, leaders who embrace their clinical roots are better equipped to navigate challenges and drive meaningful change.

Reflection Prompts:

How does your current level of clinical involvement influence your leadership style and decision-making?

What steps can you take to stay current with advancements in your clinical specialty?

How can you incorporate hands-on leadership into your current role to strengthen trust and collaboration with your team?

Actionable Steps:

4. Schedule charge shifts or shadowing opportunities to stay connected to patient care and understand team dynamics.

5. Identify one professional development opportunity, such as a certification or conference, to enhance your clinical expertise.

6. Create a plan to recognize and celebrate clinical achievements within your team, reinforcing a culture of excellence.

Notes:

_____

_____

_____

_____

_____

_____

_____

_____

_____

_____

_____

22

PREPARING FOR THE FUTURE: LEADERSHIP WITH VISION

The Importance of Vision in Leadership

Leadership is as much about preparing for tomorrow as it is about addressing today's challenges. Nurse leaders who cultivate a forward-thinking mindset position themselves and their teams to adapt, innovate, and thrive in an ever-changing healthcare landscape. A strong vision provides direction, motivates teams, and establishes a foundation for sustained success. This chapter explores the critical components of visionary leadership, including strategic planning, fostering adaptability, and preparing the next generation of nurse leaders.

Defining Your Leadership Vision

Every effective leader starts with a vision: an aspirational blueprint for the future that defines their values, goals, and aspirations. Your vision should reflect both your personal leadership philosophy and the broader mission of your organization. It's not just about dreaming big but also about aligning those dreams with actionable steps that inspire your team.

For example, a nurse leader focusing on patient safety might envision a department where zero preventable harm occurs. This vision could drive initiatives such as enhanced training programs, real-time reporting systems, and collaborative safety rounds. Similarly, a leader dedicated to fostering professional growth might prioritize creating a culture of continuous learning through mentorship, workshops, and certifications.

Articulating this vision is just as important as creating it. Share your aspirations openly with your team, outlining the path forward and the role each member plays in achieving it. Transparency fosters alignment and motivates staff to invest in shared goals.

Expanded Insight: Reflect on how your leadership vision can evolve. Visions aren't static, they grow with you and your organization. Periodically reassess your goals to ensure they remain relevant and inspiring.

Strategic Planning for the Future

Turning a vision into reality requires deliberate and strategic planning. This involves setting clear, measurable objectives, allocating resources effectively, and creating a flexible roadmap to guide implementation.

Strategic planning starts with a comprehensive assessment of your current environment. Evaluate trends in healthcare, identify challenges unique to your unit, and consider the long-term needs of your team. For instance, if emerging technologies are reshaping care delivery, a leader might develop a plan to integrate digital tools into workflows, complete with training modules and phased implementation timelines.

Leaders must also account for adaptability in their plans. Unexpected events, such as staffing shortages or policy changes, can disrupt even the best-laid strategies. Building contingency plans and maintaining regular reviews ensure that your vision stays on track, regardless of external pressures.

Fostering a Culture of Adaptability

Adaptability is a cornerstone of visionary leadership. Healthcare is inherently dynamic, and teams that embrace change are better equipped to navigate challenges and seize opportunities. Leaders play a key role in cultivating this mindset by fostering open communication, encouraging innovation, and modeling resilience.

Start by creating a safe environment where team members feel empowered to share ideas and voice concerns. Open communication lays the groundwork for adaptability by ensuring that all perspectives are considered in decision-making. Leaders should also encourage experimentation, rewarding team members who take calculated risks to improve workflows or patient outcomes.

For example, a leader facing inefficiencies in discharge procedures might invite staff to propose and test solutions. By involving the team in problem-solving, the leader not only fosters innovation but also builds confidence and ownership among staff.

Adaptability also requires a focus on emotional resilience. Provide your team with tools to manage stress and uncertainty, such as mindfulness training or peer support programs. Resilient teams are more likely to view challenges as opportunities for growth, aligning with the forward-thinking ethos of visionary leadership.

Developing the Next Generation of Nurse Leaders

A critical component of preparing for the future is cultivating new leaders. Succession planning ensures continuity and strengthens the foundation of your organization. Start by identifying staff members with leadership potential. These individuals often exhibit initiative, strong communication skills, and a commitment to professional growth.

Mentorship is a powerful tool for leadership development. Pair emerging leaders with experienced mentors who can guide them through challenges, provide feedback, and offer insights into the nuances of leadership. Structured mentorship programs, combined with opportunities for hands-on leadership roles, such as leading committees or coordinating quality improvement initiatives, prepare future leaders for success.

Expanded Insight: Leadership development isn't limited to formal programs. Informal coaching moments, such as debriefing after a challenging situation, can be just as impactful. Use these opportunities to share your thought processes and encourage reflective learning.

Building a Legacy as a Leader

Leadership is ultimately about leaving a lasting impact. Your legacy is defined by the culture you foster, the improvements you make, and the people you inspire. To build a meaningful legacy, focus on initiatives that have long-term benefits for both your team and your organization.

One way to build a legacy is by championing programs that improve patient care or enhance staff well-being. For example, implementing a mentorship initiative that continues to support new nurses long after your tenure ends creates a lasting positive effect. Leaders should also prioritize fostering a culture of professional excellence, where staff feel empowered to pursue growth and innovation.

Reflecting on your legacy throughout your leadership journey ensures intentionality in your actions. Periodic self-assessments can help you realign with your long-term goals and identify new opportunities to create meaningful change.

Leading with Vision

Visionary leadership can be described as anticipating the future and shaping it with purpose. By defining clear aspirations, creating actionable strategies, fostering adaptability, and developing future leaders, nurse leaders prepare their teams and organizations for sustained success. Leadership with vision inspires confidence, drives innovation, and leaves a legacy that impacts nursing and healthcare for years to come.

Reflection Prompts:

How does your leadership vision align with the goals of your organization and team?

_____

_____

_____

_____

_____

_____

What steps can you take to foster a culture of adaptability within your unit?

_____

_____

_____

_____

_____

_____

How can you begin mentoring and developing the next generation of nurse leaders?

_____

_____

_____

_____

_____

_____

Actionable Steps:

1. Draft a leadership vision statement and share it with your team to align efforts and inspire collaboration.

2. Develop a strategic plan to address future challenges or opportunities, incorporating input from your team.

3. Identify at least one potential leader within your team and create a tailored development plan to support their growth.

Notes:

_____

_____

_____

_____

_____

_____

_____

_____

_____

_____

_____

_____

www.ingramcontent.com/pod-product-compliance
Lightning Source LLC
Chambersburg PA
CBHW040925210326
41597CB00030B/5175